LOVING
OUT LOUD
Learning to Love
In a
Hate Filled World

Love & Blessings!

Michael DeCamp

2/14/2020

Michael DeCamp

A studybook that looks at the application of God's love through the examination of good examples, as well as the author's reflection of his own failures in demonstrating that same love.

Self Help
Christian Living

ISBN:978-1-947523-83-8

Dedication

To the man who planted the seed and set me on the course…

Ralph R. DeCamp

My father

e.

Table of Contents

Acknowledgements

This book was a compulsion. After reading my friend, Don McLaughlin's book, *Love First: Ending Hate before It's Too Late*, I found myself feeling compelled to share these stories. On top of that, I started seeing the message of love hidden in plain sight throughout the New Testament. I was driven to reevaluate how I viewed and interacted with others. Ultimately, those factors sparked me to coin a new term: *Lovementalism.*

Initially, this book was entitled *"Lovementalism: Applying Love First Concepts."* Learn more about that term within the book.

Several individuals helped me bring this compulsion to completion. First, I thank Don McLaughlin for writing the book that acted as the catalyst. He also acted as one of my beta readers. His feedback was incredibly helpful. Secondly, I thank my other beta readers: Brandi Scott-Clark, Lesha Colglazier, Dr. Greg York, and my wife, Nancy DeCamp. I'm also thankful for Dr. Patrick Mead, Dr. Jim White, Mike Runcie, and Donna

McDougall who each provided encouraging words and support. Lastly, I thank my agent, Sarah Joy Freese for her continued support.

Dear readers, it is my sincere hope that this book will be useful and helpful to you on your personal journey. May you experience the love of God in your life. In turn, may you share that love with others. Thank you for taking the time to consider the message of this book.

Foreword

You only live once, but if you do it right, once is enough. - Joe Lewis

No one wants to waste their life. Whether we know it or not, we are daily wrestling with how we spend our lives. At the heart of this struggle are two related questions: "What do I want more of?" and "What do I want less of?" These questions have concrete implications for our daily lives. Frustrated friends, struggling spouses, battling business partners, and crosswise church members all want less of what stresses them and more of what blesses them.

Even in their most distressed moments, I have never had anyone suggest they wanted more hate and less love, more judgment and less grace! Part of our deep dissatisfaction with life is rooted in our unfailing belief that the world could—and should— be a more loving place. Since more love seems to be a universal desire, why is love always struggling upstream against the rushing current of judgmentalism? The apostle Paul touched on this when he wrote to his friends in Galatia. He warned that unless they got back on track with love, they would destroy each other.[1] I'm guessing you agree: More love, less hate. More grace, less judgment.

In 2017, I went to Indianapolis to spend the weekend with my friend, Mike DeCamp. He and his church were going through my book, *Love First: Ending Hate Before It's Too Late.* He invited me to facilitate a weekend seminar to flesh out the Love First message. Mike lives life to the fullest. He is always thinking, listening, serving and writing. Mike is not paralyzed by the fear of failure or the prospect of making mistakes. He is ready to do the next right thing and learn along the journey, and he was ready to apply the Love First message to his daily life.

As we drove from the airport to the church, Mike pitched an idea to me. "What would you think if I wrote a book of stories—true stories—that illustrate Love First in action?" I was humbled and intrigued. He said. "I would title it: *Lovementalism: Applying Love First Concepts.*" He was thinking about how judgmentalism in our friendships, families, communities and churches fuels the fires of contempt, disrespect, and even hate. Judgmentalism leads to suspicion, conflict, isolation, strife, and division. We know it's bad, but what is judgmentalism?

---

[1] Galatians 5:13-14

Judgmentalism is a way of thinking—conscious and unconscious—that imagines we are justified when we embrace a negative disposition toward other people. In the Jesus way of thinking, judgmentalism is the *opposite* of the Golden Rule; it is the Greatest Command *ignored*. Judgmentalism believes there are no "Good" Samaritans, and that the sins of those we dislike should be exposed while our own sins can be explained by our good intentions and bad breaks.

Judgmentalism overstates the splinter in the eye of another while it understates the blinding beam in our own eye. Judgmentalism bashes the reputation of others while burnishing our own. It creeps into the dark crevices of our dimly lit thinking and asks, "Can anything good come out of Nazareth?" Mike knows what Jesus taught: There's only one way to have more love and less judgmentalism: You have to live the love first way every day. Mike calls this life, "Lovementalism." This is the antidote to judgmentalism.

Lovementalism is a *disposition* to love first. It is a life where love is our guiding imagination of others. Lovementalism is a commitment to patience and kindness. Lovementalism actively resists envy, boasting and pride. Yes... you guessed it... lovementalism is real love in real life.

If you agree with what you've read so far, then you are probably thinking, "Yes! But where do I begin? How do I judge less and love more? How do I overcome my prejudices and knee-jerk reactions? How do I mend broken relationships and heal hurt feelings? How do I go back to my family, work, neighborhood and church with a new perspective on those I've treated with less dignity and respect?" While I don't pretend to have all the answers, I am happy you're reading this book. Mike has compiled a series of stories from the Bible and life that offer practical direction for living love first. Mike invites you to walk with him on his own journey—mistakes and victories alike—to see one person's journey from judgmentalism to lovementalism.

So, how might you get the most from this book? First, read it like you're having coffee with a friend. Mike isn't preachy nor does he write like he has it all figured out. He's just a faithful companion. Second, look for yourself in his stories. No two people live the same life. Mike has his life and you have yours but give the challenges at the close of each chapter a try. Create your own lovementalism experiences. Maybe not everything will translate from his story to yours but take his principles and put them to work. And finally, Mike writes from his heart. You will receive the greatest blessing if you read from the heart. His stories breathe passion, humility, and insight. Only an open heart can receive what is shared from the heart.

I am blessed to know Mike as a friend and brother in Christ. His journey from judgmentalism is authentic. You and I are both blessed to join him on this journey to lovementalism.

Don McLaughlin
Author of *Love First: Ending Hate Before It's Too Late*
ACU Press - 2017

LOVING OUT LOUD

Introduction

From Concept to Reality

One of my earliest memories of my Dad is of him holding me on his chest one night. We were in the front bedroom of our two-bedroom home. I remember how the furniture was arranged. It's like it is locked into my memory bank. As I think about that moment, I can still almost smell his cologne. He held me, and he spoke to me, whispering in my ear. I'm sure he had a lot to say, but I only remember one thing.

"Mike, the most important thing that you can do in your life is love God."

It was a simple thing, and many people would likely think that it wouldn't mean much to a toddler whose main focus in life at the time was probably trying to figure out the purpose of his own toes.

However, they would be wrong. Those simple words whispered into my young ear have been the guiding force in my life from that day until today. I think that is what my dad intended and hoped.

I only wish I could live up to them.

My dad's message is a truncation of Jesus' words found, among other places, in the Gospel of Matthew.

Jesus replied: "'Love the Lord your God with all your heart and with all your soul and with all your mind' This is the first and greatest commandment." Matthew 22:37-38 (NIV)

Over the years, I've heard parents discuss the importance of teaching their children about the Bible and about going to church. They drill them on the various books of the Bible and on the various stories from Genesis to the Revelation. Adam and Eve. Abraham and Isaac. Jacob and Esau. Noah's Ark. David and Goliath. Samson. Jonah and the whale. Jesus walking on the water. All of these people and events are important, but we cannot miss the heart of the matter because the whole thing is one big love story: God's love for us, and his desire that we love him back. *"For God so loved the world that he gave…"* really is a big deal of the biggest kind.

As key as my Dad's message was to my youthful mind, he didn't include another vital part of the message in his initial life lesson to me. Jesus had a "Part Two" in his message in Matthew.

"And the second is like it: 'Love your neighbor as yourself.'" Matthew 22:39 (NIV)

My Dad was not a theologian. He wasn't even a

church-attender. Somehow, though, along the course of his life and his personal, daily Bible study, he had gleaned the bottom line. Loving God was not just a nice idea. It was THE idea. He shared that directly to my impressionable ear. The second part was something he shared more subtly—more through how he treated others and expected me to act with respect to those around me.

I wish I could say that my Dad was the perfect example, but that is just not the case. Sometimes he was harsh. Sometimes he said things that hurt me. He made mistakes. Even so, I don't resent those shortfalls. After all, we all learn, grow, and act imperfectly. I'm just grateful that he set my life's foundation on the true rock. Now, it is up to me to build the rest of the house.

With that foundation, I did set out to build my spiritual house. Through the influence of a neighbor, I began to attend church and found a spiritual family. A couple of youth ministers provided important direction through my dangerous teen years. When I graduated from high school, I decided to pursue more biblical education and went off to attend a Bible college in West Virginia. After that, I began to pursue certain styles of ministry that seemed devoted and successful. Along the way, I've taken detours down various paths: Doctrine, Politics, Being in the Right Church, Discipleship, Legalism, Conservatism, Liberalism—you name it. With every one of those roads, I've come up short. Something always seemed to be missing. Sure, along the way, I've learned some vital concepts like grace, forgiveness, and reliance on God, but more and more, I started to feel like there was another basic ingredient missing in my life. And, not just my life. It seemed to be missing in the faith communities that surrounded me.

Now, here I am in the second half of my life (assuming a normal lifespan) and I've circled back around to those words my Dad whispered into my ear. "Love God." Further, I've learned to enhance those words with the second half of the scripture. "Love your neighbor."

Jesus added: *"All the Law and the Prophets hang on these two commandments."* Matthew 22:40 (NIV)

If we don't get this right, nothing else matters. Trying to be a Christian without a focus on learning to love is like trying to make bread without any flour or like trying to swim in a pool without any water.

Bob Goff, in his book *Love Does*, taught me that love is more than a nice feeling. It is an action. It is what you do. It is how you live. Don McLaughlin, in his book *Love First*, taught me that love should be at the core of everything we do as Christians— both personally and corporately. These works have driven me to look at the scriptures in a deeper way, and as a result, I've found love. It really is everywhere in the Bible. Even in passages where it isn't directly mentioned, it is at the core of the message. It is like the blinders have come off or scales have fallen from my eyes and I can finally see. I still remember in fourth grade when I got my first pair of glasses. My parents thought they'd have a hard time getting me to wear them, but boy were they wrong. As I put them on, a whole new world appeared before my eyes. That's how I feel about reading the Bible these days. I'm seeing a whole new level of message sitting there right on top.

What I hope to do in this book is give you practical examples to consider. I am going to approach it from two angles. On the one hand, I will share personal examples where people have truly exemplified a spirit of love (*agape*) in how they have treated me. On the other hand, I am going to share with you examples where I totally missed the mark—ways that I failed to show love. Hopefully, you can glean insight from those examples while considering others from your own life. Together, perhaps we can reform a spirit of love in our lives, our churches, and our communities as a whole. I want to take the concepts I've been learning and make them reality.

Finally, in chapter sixteen, I will to introduce you to *Lovementalism*. It is a state of mind—a way of thinking. It is something that you have to train yourself to do—a mental discipline that incorporates the message of the scripture into the way that we see and approach those around us.

Let's see where this "love thing" takes us. Let's go on a journey together. Maybe we can even change the trajectory of our world while we're at it.

One

Kristi's Friend

Meaningful Words and a Hurtful Tongue

Therefore if you have any encouragement from being united with Christ, if any comfort from his love, if any common sharing in the Spirit, if any tenderness and compassion, then make my joy complete by being like-minded, having the same love, being one in spirit and of one mind. Do nothing out of selfish ambition or vain conceit. Rather, in humility value others above yourselves, not looking to your own interests but each of you to the interests of others. Philippians 2:1-4 (NIV)

I wish I could invent a way to tie a string to the words I say so that if I say something stupid, hurtful, or offensive, I could just pull them back in before anyone hears. If only I had a magic reset button that I could hit to erase the last five seconds and I could start over. Have you ever felt that way? If I could invent either of those, I bet you'd buy them. I bet I'd become so rich that I could buy out Warren Buffet. Instead of the Oracle of Omaha, I'd be the Oracle of Indy.

One day not all that long ago, I was sitting in a class on Sunday morning at church when one of those moments came around. A friend of mine was sharing a lengthy comment on the subject we were discussing when all at once a horn began to sound outside. It kept going off while my friend continued to share. The two sounds conflicted for several more seconds. Finally, some of the guys jumped up to see what the noise outside was all about. As it turns out, it wasn't much of anything important, so everyone came back to their seats. Someone said everything was under control, but I said:

"I thought it was just someone trying to get (my friend) to stop talking."

Folks laughed. I think my friend even laughed. He didn't seem to be overly bothered, but immediately I wished I had not spoken. I wished that I had the ability to reel the words right back in or hit the reset button. If only I could just hit backspace in real life.

Words are powerful things. Words have consequences. Words can change things—for good or ill. Think Lincoln and the Gettysburg Address. Think Dr. Martin Luther King Jr. and his "I Have a Dream" speech. Think Hitler in pre-WWII Germany. **Good or ill.**

Words matter.

That event from Sunday reminded me of a story from my days in the church youth group as a teen in Muncie, Indiana. I was probably a senior in high school at the time and I was regarded as a leader among the teens. I should have known better than to do what I did.

I was someone that the youth leader, Neil, had identified as a person with whom he would personally work to develop as an asset to the group. On an intellectual level, I understood that he loved and respected me, and that my teen group friends loved me as well, but often my insecurities took control. You see, at my core, I was deeply insecure in nearly all circumstances. It made me hyper-sensitive and even sometimes a little suspicious. Generally, I covered it up by trying to be funny. If I could make the other teens laugh, then I felt appreciated and liked. I sought to win the other teens' approval through their laughter. Usually, those attempts at humor were harmless—although I suspect they were likely quite obnoxious too. Still, there was one time when I said something so horrible in an ill-fated attempt to provoke laughter that I still cringe when I think about it to this day. I really should have known better.

It was "Monday Night Fellowship." That was our youth group's weekly teen event. It was held at a different family's home each time we met, but I don't recall where we were that particular week. We all loved those nights together. We had so much fun playing games, singing songs, and learning from our youth minister's devotionals. We laughed and joked and cut up. I have so many memories from those days. Wow. That group made my teen years bearable.

Monday Night Fellowship was also the one event where we could bring friends and be assured that they would have a good time. They could connect with our group, hear a message from scripture in a relaxed atmosphere, and walk away encouraged. It was an outreach event for our group and it wasn't uncommon for new kids to show up on any given Monday.

On the night of my big mouth, Kristi had brought a friend, a girl from her school. In general, I remember that she was very friendly, and out-going, and sort of cute. However, she had one rather prominent feature that was overtly apparent to everyone in the room. Fortunately almost everyone had the good sense to keep their mouths shut and their thoughts to themselves. Almost everyone.

Everyone but me. I had no good sense about me on that particular night.

During the devotional, Neil, the youth minister was sharing a message. I don't recall the overall gist, but in the message we were asked to say something encouraging about someone else in the room. The point was to learn to build one another up in a positive way. In one incredible example of my own thick-headedness, I completely missed that point.

"Look around the room," he said. "Share something encouraging about someone."

Enter me—and my personal insecurities blanketed in a need to be funny.

I looked around for someone to share about. Simultaneously, my brain was working on some creative way to be funny, to make everyone laugh. It had taken that opportunity to build someone else up and converted it into an opportunity to ease those lingering insecurities—to build itself up. I spotted the cute, out-going, visiting girl with the prominent feature. She was sitting there, looking comfortable with the group, listening to the message, engaged, and enjoying the experience. With impeccable timing, I got everyone's attention, pointed and said: "She has a big nose!"

Looking back, I just don't understand how I could say something like that. Why would I put the need to be funny so far ahead of any sense of common decency? Why would I even think that *was* funny? How could I be so hurtful? Was it some sort of twisted, adolescent attempt at flirting? I am still ashamed to this very moment.

The room went dead silent in shock for what seemed like eons but was probably only about long enough for Neil to connect his brain to his mouth and say: *"THAT WAS UNCALLED FOR! I DON'T WANT TO HEAR ANYTHING LIKE THAT FROM YOU EVER AGAIN!"*

My shame was immediate, deep, and deserved. For the rest of the evening, I withdrew into myself out of complete humiliation. I can't recall if I ever apologized. I sure hope I did, but that wouldn't have made the girl's pain and embarrassment any less. I had taken an innocent stranger and trampled on her for my own benefit.

Here's the thing. I never saw that girl again.

That, maybe, is the worst thing about what I did. My words severed the potential of relationships between that girl and our group and our church. Perhaps we could have been great friends, but my words spoiled it all. I had humiliated her. Who knows what lasting effects that event had? Who knows what the downstream consequences have been?

Words are powerful. Words matter.

In the Bible, in the book of James, the writer says: ***Those who consider themselves religious and yet do not keep a tight rein on their tongues deceive themselves, and their religion is worthless.*** James 1:26 (NIV)

That evening, I made my religion worthless. I traded the faith I believed in and the Lord I served for what I had hoped would be a few seconds of reassuring laughter. I wonder how often our religious words have a similar effect on folks as my thoughtless words had on that girl so many years ago. How often do we sever a person's connection to the church through our need to be right or our need to get our point across? How often do our flippant words disconnect people from our body of believers? Do we trade our faith and the deep wealth of opportunity that relationships hold for a few seconds of making our point?

Obviously, from the story I told at the outset of this chapter, I have not yet mastered my mouth. Unfortunately, I still have a tendency to want the approval of others that can be found in their laughter, and that need comes out occasionally in a rather sharp, sarcastic manner. I am a work in progress, but my highest goal these days is to use my words in meaningful ways. To help and not to harm. To build up and not to tear down.

I like to think that I follow that positive course much more now than I did in my past.

Do not let any unwholesome talk come out of your mouths, but only what is helpful for building others up according to their needs, that it may benefit those who listen. Ephesians 4:29 (NIV)

I was thinking about the story of my hurtful words recently while perusing the vast amount of words bantered around on Facebook and Twitter. This person hates that public figure. That person is standing up against that terrible social wrong, which someone else hatefully argues is a social right. There's another vulgar joke, another false accusation, another profanity-laced political rant against this group or that group. Many of the words are strong, but how many are truly meaningful and meant to build up rather than to tear down? How many are meant to show love to one another? You be the judge.

If I had the chance today to stand in humility before that girl from so many years ago, I would tell her how sorry I truly am. May I NEVER again have the need to apologize like that to anyone, but the chances are that I will. The key to any potential success I may have, though, is likely found in those words I shared at the outset of this chapter—the words from Philippians 2: *Do nothing out of selfish ambition or vain conceit. Rather, in humility value others above yourselves, not looking to your own interests but each of you to the interests of others.*

(NIV) This passage is a description of biblical love—the unselfish nature of *agape* love put into practice. More and more, as I grow in my love for others, my insecurities have less and less space to operate. If I had understood that concept more fully as a teen, perhaps I would have at least one more friend in my life today.

Your words have power. Your words matter. Be meaningful, helpful, and encouraging to someone **with your words** every chance you get. You really can make a positive difference in someone's life.

The world can be moved with strong, loving, meaningful words; yours and mine. **Be mindful of your power—the power of *agape* love put into practice.**

Discussion Questions

1. Share about a time when you said something that you wished you could immediately reel back in.
2. Can you think of a famous quote that has touched you in some personal way? Please share.
3. How have insecurities (either yours or someone else's) had an impact on your relationship(s)?
4. Read Philippians 2:1-4. How can this verse change the dynamic of our everyday interactions?
5. In light of Philippians 2:1-4 and Ephesians 4:29, how should Christians temper their words on social media sites?

Challenge

Apologize to someone for something you should not have said. Also, go out of your way to say something encouraging—build someone up with your words.

Two

Donny, Marie, and LeBron

Real People, Real Words

Love... It does not dishonor others,... I Corinthians 13:5 (NIV)

Those who consider themselves religious and yet do not keep a tight rein on their tongues deceive themselves, and their religion is worthless. James 1:26 (NIV)

So in everything, do to others what you would have them do to you, for this sums up the Law and the Prophets. Matthew 7:12 (NIV)

Recently, my wife and I took a trip to Las Vegas. It was one of those in-and-out kind of quick trips. It had one primary purpose: see Donny Osmond live at the show he and his sister do at the Flamingo Hotel before they finally close it out and end their run. Mission accomplished!

My wife has been a fan of Donny Osmond since she was a very young girl. Personally, I've always been more of a Marie fan. In my opinion, she's just cuter. (Sorry, Donny, but you know it's true.) When Nancy mentioned to me a few months ago that the Donny and Marie show in Vegas would soon be coming to a close after over a decade of performances, I told her we should go. She said, "Really?" I said, "Sure." So, we did.

Nancy ordered VIP tickets. As a result, not only did we get to attend the show, but we also sat on the front row. We could reach out and touch the stage. Nancy was excited! I was, too. We were so close that a few splatters of Marie's sweat actually landed on Nancy. I was kind of jealous.

Not only did we sit on the front row, but the VIP tickets also allowed us the opportunity to attend an after-show meet and greet. We had the opportunity to meet both Donny and Marie. We shook their hands and had pictures taken; I have the pictures to prove it. Actual real words were exchanged. It was amazing. Would you believe that they are both real living, breathing human beings?

Do you know what you learn when you get to do something like that? You learn that those people that you've been watching on that little TV screen or up on the big movie screen or following on that digital device (Twitter, Facebook, Instagram, etc.), well, they are actual, real people. They have skin. They have actual hands and feet. They get out of breath. They sweat—and sometimes it splatters on you.

And, they have feelings.

I know it's hard to believe but they have real, honest to goodness feelings.

The show was about an hour and a half long, but the meet and greet lasted for more than two hours, maybe three. Those two lifelong entertainers spent the entire time shaking hands, taking pictures, and talking. Really talking. They answered questions and listened to people's stories.

At one point, while Nancy and I stood in line with two hundred of our closest friends that we'd never before met, one woman was pulled from far back in the line so that she could sit down and wait for the line to catch up to her. She was just too weak to stand up that long. Donny saw her and when he finished with the person he had been greeting, he went to her, sat down, and just connected. As her story went, she had recently lost her daughter, who was supposed to join her on the trip. Instead, she was there with her sister and she was clearly still in mourning. Donny spent a long time just talking with her and trying to console her. Later, she went further down the line and Marie did the same thing. It was impressive to watch, but they didn't do it to impress. I believe they did it because they are real people and were connecting with another real person who was in pain. They allowed themselves to experience compassion.

There is an odd thing in our modern media-driven society. Famous people are so much in front of us that we seem to stop believing they are real.

They are like characters in a book that have come to life, but still aren't real. We think they are just a thing of fiction. It doesn't matter what we say to them or how we treat them, they are celluloid, plastic, synthetic beings without feelings or a right to privacy. Their pain means nothing to us.

I have been as prone to this malady as anyone. My hometown NBA team, the Pacers were playing LeBron James' team, the Cleveland Cavaliers, a while back and I got all caught up in the emotion of the moment. I've never been a LeBron fan and that's okay. I don't have to be a fan of opposing players. I suppose if he ended up playing in Indiana, my heart would soften toward him. It's only natural. As it stands, though, I just don't cheer for him, even though I recognize his incredible talent.

As the situation unfolded, the Pacers had battled his team tooth and nail. They had put up a valiant fight but had fallen in defeat. LeBron had done what he does so often; he had turned on the afterburners and blasted them into submission. I was heartbroken and dejected. I was angry and looking for a target at which I could shoot my daggers of emotion.

I lashed out.

Basically, I took to Twitter and said something very negative about LeBron. I even hash-tagged him. I intended for anyone who follows him, perhaps even LeBron himself, to see it. In fact, I truly hoped he would see it. I wanted to take the air out of his victory balloon.

At first, I thought I was clever. I'm an author and I had strung together some clever words, saying something mean-spirited cloaked inside some insincere compliments. The compliments were really just back-handed jabs at his character. Boy, did I tell him.

I had a problem, though. The problem was that I had recently become obsessed with loving people the way God wanted me to do it. Therefore, I knew that doing what I had done did not fit that expectation and goal. I knew that I was being mean-spirited and wasn't following the command to love my neighbor. My conscience rebelled against my clever words.

LeBron probably never saw the tweet. If he did, he probably just blew it off. After all, he likely gets thousands of tweets coming at him in a constant barrage. Still, I knew what I had done, and I knew it was inappropriate, unloving, and just plain wrong. The more I thought about it, the more guilty I felt. I couldn't cope with the inconsistency between what I knew to be right and the reality of my action. Eventually, I did the only thing I could do. Since I couldn't untweet it, I hash-tagged him again, this time with an apology. I knew it had to be done. He probably never saw that either, but God did.

For one heated moment, I forgot that LeBron James is a real person with a family, a heart, and feelings.

Politicians are another category of people that we seem to have lost any sense of their humanity. As I write this, we are about to enter another heated political season. Politics has always been an ugly business, but over the last several years, it seems that the ugliness has reached an all-time high. Social media has made everyone into a pundit and a talking head. Memes have taken the place of newspapers and magazines. TV news is all about opinion and that gets amplified as it gets copied and pasted into every social site around. Add in the fake messages and you've got the witch's brew for demonizing anyone brave enough to run for public office.

Here's my message to you, whether you are reading this within the cycle that is currently starting or find yourself in some future political cycle, please remember that the person you are tempted to attack is a real person. He or she has a family. They probably have children. They breath and eat and sleep. They are sometimes right, and they are sometimes wrong—just like the rest of us. They have feelings and a heart. They can be just as incredibly injured by hateful words and messages as you or I.

I have sometimes forgotten that in my rush to defend or promote my own personal views.

We can justify ourselves by pointing to what we believe to be their immoral positions on social issues or their lack of integrity or even their loose grasp on the truth. Those factors may or may not be true, but whether they are or not is on them. As a Christ-follower, my obligation it to someone higher and I must follow His higher expectation.

As a Christ-follower, I am obligated to love (*agape*) them—even if they are my political enemy. I am obligated to treat them the way that I'd want to be treated if I were in their shoes. I am obligated to keep a tight rein on my tongue.

It is one thing to disagree, but it is another thing

altogether to disparage and say hateful things—especially in a public forum. I have a favor to ask. Please join me in not cloaking our hateful words inside a blanket of pseudo-Christian piety. To do so is to dishonor our Lord.

During the last cycle, I found one side effect of all the hateful posts and memes especially distressing. There were young Christians who, because of those hateful words, lost their respect for older Christians, the very people who had been formative in their early faith walk. Some of those young people have walked away from their spiritual families altogether, perhaps even from God, disillusioned and at a loss to find a place to connect. When I consider this, some words of Jesus come to my mind. They have to do with causing the young to stumble and millstones around the neck and being cast into the sea. Check out Matthew 18:6-7.

Personally, I have decided to make it my practice to avoid saying anything negative against any individual, in the public eye or not, on any kind of public forum. I no longer post political rants, nor do I participate in social media debates. Sure, I have the right to freedom of speech. I have the right to share my political views. I have an obligation to participate in our democracy. Still, I have a much greater obligation and that obligation is to love. To love my enemies. To love my neighbor. To love my family. To love those people who may be observing my attitudes and actions. And, by extension, to love even those people who don't quite seem real to me because they are always in the public eye. I have an obligation to treat them the way that I'd want to be treated.

One concept that I adopted in 2016: I care more about my friendships, my relationships, and people in general than I do about my opinions. I hope you agree.

Discussion Questions

1. Have you ever met a famous person? What about them seemed normal to you?
2. Why do you think we find it so easy to say hateful things on social media?
3. Have you ever felt disillusioned by something someone said on social media?
4. Discuss the merits of either disconnecting from social media or trying to view it as a mission field. Should we withdraw from this cultural phenomenon or try to engage in a positive way?
5. What are the potential negative side effects of engaging in religious or political debates on social media?

Challenge

For the next week, purposefully avoid making negative social media posts and, instead, intentionally post only positive comments—at least one per day—directed toward someone who needs encouragement.

Three

Emma

Making a Difference,
One Family at a Time

"Love your neighbor as yourself." Jesus in Luke 10:27 (NIV)

But he wanted to justify himself, so he asked Jesus, "And who is my neighbor?" Luke 10:29 (NIV)

Jesus used this interaction as a springboard into the famous story of the Good Samaritan. He gave us this parable to show us that your neighbor is whoever has a need and is within your reach. Go give them what you would need, if you were in their shoes. Maybe even give them your shoes.

Recently, I was thinking about the concept of neighbors in our modern society. I know this has been said before by someone, but we seem to have become an incredibly unsocial society in the age of *social* media. When I was a child, we actually knew our neighbors. We visited them. We borrowed sugar or milk—we really did. We had no air-conditioning, so it was standard practice to sit outside in the evenings and visit with the folks next door, who were doing the same. Privacy fences had not become a thing yet, so we could see and interact with one another. We had three and a half TV channels, so there really wasn't much to watch— especially during the summer rerun season.

Today, we sit inside our air-conditioned homes, watching our huge screen televisions with hundreds of viewing choices, or playing with our smart phones. We play *Words with Friends* with people we can't see instead of going over and sharing real words with real people. If we do go outside, we huddle behind our large privacy fences, scrolling social media and keeping our distance from the faces on the other side.

I can understand the desire for that separation. Dealing with people can make for some complications and difficult interactions. Being involved with real people can be messy. Take my own family, for example.

In the mid to late 1960's, the DeCamp household on South Hackley Street in Muncie, Indiana was no stranger to drama. I was a child, so I was more or less oblivious. I didn't know any better. My assumption was that all families were like mine.

When my mother gave me birth, I had three siblings from my mom's previous marriage. The closest one had just turned sixteen about two weeks before I was born. My sister was seventeen and my oldest brother was nineteen. That was December of 1961.

By the end of the 60's decade, my oldest brother had been married twice with two children, one of which died as an infant. He had been in and out of the county jail many times. He would have been twenty-seven, but he ended up killing himself in 1969 during an argument with his second wife—in my sister's kitchen. He had failed in two previous attempts to take his own life, but this one succeeded. My sister had been married and divorced as a teenager and was living as a single mother on her own at the time my oldest brother died. The youngest of my brothers had been to prison for a couple of years and was struggling with a difficult marriage, also. There is a lot more, but let's just say that all of this spilled in and out of our Hackley Street home on a regular basis.

I remember trips to the county jail to visit one or both of my brothers. I remember talk of stolen cars, fights, bail bonds and lawyers. To this day, there is a bullet hole in the aluminum siding in the corner of my parent's former home. It was put there by one of my brothers—I don't recall which.

All of that was on top of the everyday activities that included lots of arguing and cursing, lots of slammed doors and squealing tires. It must have been an experience to live next door to our family.

So late in that turbulent decade, when Emma moved in next door with her young family, I'm sure we must have presented quite a challenge to her.

She was a young, twenty-something Christian mother with two children and I have no doubt that our free-for-all family must have been daunting, to say the least. Keep in mind, we had no air-conditioning, so anything that was said, yelled, or cursed inside our home was clearly heard by anyone nearby—especially on Emma's side of our house. If they existed at the time, it must have occurred to her to put up a big privacy fence to block out our mess. There really would have been no other way to avoid us. Her home was one half of a double and literally all her windows opened toward our house—only about thirty feet away. Winter must have provided some much-needed peace and quiet.

Maybe it was a temptation for her to shun us. Maybe she considered ways that she could limit her children's exposure to us. I can imagine her begging her husband to find a different house. She could have huddled them inside while our family was coming and going. She could have avoided talking to any of us. She could have slammed the door in my six-year-old face when I tapped on it to ask for a cookie.

She didn't do any of that.

Rather than find ways to avoid and block us out, she befriended my mother—which, by the way, was no easy task. I love my mother, but she could be difficult. Still, Emma reached out. I was a couple of years older than her kids, but we played together. I don't remember them at our house much, but I was always welcome at their house. My mother had several stays in the hospital during those years, especially after my brother died, and Emma would visit.

Emma became especially important in my life. She actually said no to my first cookie request, but after that, it was all smooth-sailing. As I mentioned, she welcomed my friendship with her kids. She took me to Vacation Bible School in the summer. She and her husband even took me with them on a family vacation to Tennessee. As an urban kid, I have to say, that was a memorable trip—cows, corn, horses, barns, chickens, and fresh (and I do mean fresh) milk and butter. I especially remember the chocolate gravy and biscuits—delicious!

After my brother's death in 1969, my mother's health really took a negative turn, driven by the grief, sorrow, and depression. As I have already mentioned, she had several more hospital stays, some in the psychiatric wing. It was during one of those stays that Emma's outreach began to pay dividends. She had arranged for her minister, Ron Miller, to make contact with my mom. Now, I don't recall if he simply called, or if he made some visits to the hospital. I think it likely that he actually visited. Either way, he became a resource for my mother to share and release some of her pain.

Ron's talks with my mother led to the church youth minister, Mike Runcie, reaching out to me. Mike dangled some pretty attractive prizes in front of me. If I started riding the bus to church, their youth group had a lot of fun activities: summer church camp, Cincinnati Reds games, and trips to Kings Island—a local amusement park. He pretty much rang all my bells.

"What time will the bus pick me up?" I asked.

Soon, I was going to church every Sunday. A couple of years later, I got involved with other youth group functions. As a teen, I made a commitment to Christ and my closest friends were in my youth group. At the age in which my brothers were stealing cars, fighting, and discovering alcohol, I was going to church, learning about God, and setting a different course for my life. Our family trajectory changed.

All because Emma loved her neighbors.

That young, Christian mother changed the trajectory of our family because she was willing to follow Christ's directive to *love your neighbor*. My life would be very, very different today, if she had withheld that love. After all, the odds were heavily against me.

Years later, after Emma had passed away, I was able to help my Uncle come to faith, and shortly after that, my mother finally accepted the grace of God in her life. I baptized her when she was eighty-one years old—about four months before she passed away. These two wonderful events trace back to Emma's choice to reach out.

I'm far from a perfect man, but I have a wonderful family with two fantastic daughters, and I serve my local congregation as an elder. Again, this would be so highly unlikely if not for Emma loving her neighbors.

The interesting thing is that her actions did not yield some big splash at the time. For years, there were no appreciable results. Then, all she got was this neighbor kid going to church on Sundays. Still, the downstream effect has been exponentially larger—and continues to expand. For one thing, you are reading this book because Emma loved her neighbors.

Don't underestimate the power and effect of following the simple command to love your neighbors. Take a look at that struggling family next door. Ignore the unkempt grass, the curse words, and the slamming doors. Let your heart reach past your privacy fence. Step over the empty beer cans and make contact. Put down the phone and the remote and go pick up the future of a hurting soul. You just might change someone's life trajectory. That little splash might have ripples that will span decades.

Discussion Questions

1. How many of your physical neighbors do you really know? What are the obstacles in getting to know them?
2. What makes loving your neighbor a daunting command?
3. What are the cultural influences that make it more difficult to connect with those nearby?
4. Do you ever feel lonely? Could others be feeling the same way?
5. Can you share an example of the ripple effect of someone loving a neighbor?
6. What can you do to make a difference in a neighbor's life?

Challenge

Make some cookies (or buy them) and take them to your actual next door neighbors. Introduce yourself. Make a new friend.

Four

Jean

Love is an Action
Word

Love never fails. 1 Corinthians 13:8 (NIV)
"It works every time it's tried." John Wright

The problem is that I don't always—or even often—try it. I don't know about you, but I am way too often oblivious to what is going on around me, and sometimes it really is a problem. I remember sitting in a fast food restaurant one icy winter day and as I munched on my burger, I was staring through the window at the sun reflecting off of the wintery slick pavement. There was something going on, but my mind was in my own little world. I registered movement, but I was oblivious as to what it was or what it meant. It was only after three or four other men jumped to their feet and rushed out the door that I realized that what I was staring at was a woman who had fallen on the ice and was struggling to get up. I sat in my seat feeling a touch guilty as those men helped her to her feet and led her into the restaurant. She wasn't injured, but I felt rather worthless.

Biblical love is an action word. One of the issues in our modern, western world is that we confuse love with an emotion. We think to love someone is to feel warm feelings about them. I call it the "warm and fuzzies." The truth is that you can love someone biblically and really not like them at all. You're probably scratching your head right now. Huh? How can that be? The vast majority of the occasions where love is mentioned in the New Testament it is translated from the ancient Greek word *agape*. There are other ancient Greek words that are sometimes used, but *agape* is, by far, the word that is associated with Christian love. The thing about *agape* is that it is about what you do and not about what you feel. Or, it is about what you choose and not how you feel about that choice. I can choose to do good to or for someone regardless of how I feel about them. I can choose to seek the best for my friend, my neighbor, or my enemy without the presence of any affection at all. That is how Jesus could command us to love our enemies. He didn't necessarily mean that we need to feel all warm and fuzzy on the inside. Rather, we need to seek to do good to them and for them. By doing so, we love (*agape*) them. If you get the warm and fuzzies along the way, count it as a bonus.

When someone needs respect and we give it—we have loved them.

When someone needs money and we provide it—we have loved them.

When someone needs a listening ear and we listen—we have loved them.

When someone needs help around their home and we assist them—we have loved them.

When someone is belittled and oppressed, and we defend and uplift them—we have loved them.

When we do nothing but sit in our recliner and think warm thoughts about various people, but never take any positive action toward them—despite how we may feel, we haven't loved them—not even a little. If I claim to love my brother, but I leave him high and dry when he needs my help, then I'm lying—to myself, to my brother, and to my God.

Now, back to my oblivious nature. A number of years ago, my wife and I opened up our home to Brandy, a young, single mother with three children. They stayed with us (my wife and I and our two daughters) in our three-bedroom house for several weeks. It was crowded, but we made the best of it. That's the backdrop. One evening, my wife said something—I don't recall what—and I replied: "You never told me that!" Now, this was an ongoing thing with us. My wife would bring something up that she had supposedly already mentioned to me, but I would not remember anything about it. I was convinced that she was wrong, that she had never mentioned it; that perhaps she only thought she told me. This event was a repeat of that old scenario. The problem was that this time, my wife had a witness.

I said, "You never said that!"

Immediately, Brandy interjected: "Yes, she did. You were sitting right there, and she was standing over there, and she said…"

I was busted in my obliviousness. I didn't love my wife by giving her my full attention. Rather, I had obviously zoned out into my own world and had not been paying attention to her. I wish I could say that I immediately changed, but that is not the case. I continue to work on it, but sometimes I find that my world is no bigger than the space behind my eyeballs. I get sucked into my selfish mind. Still, at least I'm aware of the truth now.

Fast forward a few years. I'm sitting in my home office during the work week and I'm working on some issue, plan, or need for my employer—I don't recall what it was. I was very busy and probably under a time crunch. My mind was fully engaged, and it was consuming my thought energy. My phone rings—a distraction—so I yank my brain out of the task at hand and pick it up.

"Hello?" I said.

"Mike, this is Bill," the voice on the phone said. Bill was my friend. He was a number of years older than me, but we had grown to be friends over the years of being in the same church and the same ministries. He and his wife, Jean, were in our small group. I was leading that group and was responsible for the care and nurturing of the members.

"Hi Bill," I said. "What's up?"

"Mike, Jean's brother has died. We're headed

over to Illinois now. Can you make sure that the church knows? She's going to need prayers and encouragement."

"Sure," I said. "I'll let them know." Bill and I exchanged a few more words. I got the details and then we hung up. I needed to call some folks to let them know, but decided to do it later—after I'd gotten my work done. The next thing I knew, I was again fully engrossed in my consuming project. I allowed myself to be sucked back in behind my own eyeballs.

I never called anyone. It had completely flown out of my mind.

Sunday rolled around and I see Bill at church. No announcement was made about Jean's loss. No one called her. No one supported her in her time of need. Why? It was because I failed to love my sister in the faith. I had gotten pulled back into my personal world and left her out to dry. Bill was livid. Angry is too soft of a word. I had allowed his beloved wife to suffer in her grief without her church family's support. If you ever have wondered how Peter felt when that rooster crowed, look into your friend's eyes right after you realize that you've truly let them down. What he said to me cut me to my core.

"Bill, I am so, so sorry," I said. "Please forgive me."

"I don't think I'll ever be able to forgive you for this," he replied. They were not hollow words. He meant them.

I was devastated. Heartbroken. I had been worthless to Bill and Jean and I felt worthless to the rest of the small group, and to God, as well.

A lack of love had severely wounded our relationship—<u>my</u> lack of love. Love itself had not failed, but, rather, I had failed to try love, to apply love. I had not applied *agape* love. If I had truly loved Bill and Jean, I would have taken care of them in their hour of need.

I will say, though, that love did ultimately come through in the end. Bill and Jean both forgave me. They loved me, and love did work because Bill tried it even despite my failure. As a result of my guilt and broken heart over my failure to love Jean, I stepped away from my leadership of the small group. In a sense, I gave up. I had let two people down that I held great affection for and had failed to love them. However, instead of holding on to their pain and hurt, my friends reached out to me and forgave me, encouraging me to not give up on what God could do with me.

"Don't be obsessed with getting your own advantage. Forget yourselves long enough to lend a helping hand." Philippians 2:3-4 (The Message)

One of my greatest faults is a tendency to get lost in my own mind. I get oblivious to the people around me. This is selfishness, something that 1 Corinthians 13:5 says that love is not. However, I don't think I'm alone in this. Do you? Maybe there is a reason that the Bible spends so much time and so many words trying to explain to us the value of *agape* love.

My friend, John Wright says of love: "It works every time it's tried." Let's keep trying.

Discussion Questions

1. Do things sometimes go "in one ear and out the other" when someone speaks to you? Can you share an example?
2. Can you share about a time when you were oblivious to what was happening around you?
3. Have you ever been hurt because someone was oblivious to your obvious need? Please share, but be careful not to confess someone else's sin.
4. Have you tried loving them with forgiveness?
5. Can you think of any needs around you to which you can actively respond?
6. What are some difficult situations where love can be tried?

Challenge

Take time this week to look around at the people nearby. This could be anywhere. It could be at lunch, in your office or class, or even in the supermarket. Consider the needs you can observe by simply paying attention.

Five

Delores

A Term Paper and Washed Feet

Carry each other's burdens, and in this way you will fulfill the law of Christ. Galatians 6:2 (NIV)

"A new command I give you: Love one another. As I have loved you, so you must love one another." John 13:34 (NIV)

A few years ago, I was asked to lead a devotional for teenagers at our church's family camp. As the devo approached, I gathered a couple of items and placed them in the center of a circle of chairs: a pan of water and a towel. They were in the middle so everyone would see them. After all the teens gathered and the singing ended, it was time for my message. The first thing I did was have them count off—one, two, one, two—all the way around the circle. "Okay," I said, "Now, I want all of the twos to take off your shoes and socks. Then, turn your Bibles to John 13."

I bet you think you know where I went and what I had them do. If you are a student of the scriptures, you know that John 13 is the passage where Jesus washed the disciples' feet. Those teens were pretty sure that was where I was going, and it got kind of uncomfortable in the room. Touching someone's feet is sort of invading personal space, and not really a pleasant idea. Plus, not all of the young people were sitting beside others that they were even remotely close to, at least not on both sides. As I looked around, I saw sheepish looks and a good deal of squirming. I had water. I had towels. I had bare feet. I had half the kids remove their shoes, so the obvious assumption was that the other half would do the washing. I walked right up to it, right up to the edge.

Nope. I didn't do it. You see, foot-washing is a voluntary thing. For service to others to have a heart-changing effect, it has to be done out of freewill and a sense of love. That was my ultimate point. I explained that to the teens gathered around that basin and even the air felt thinner as the tension dissipated. Still, I hope the group understood the lesson; that Jesus expects us to freely choose to love.

In the spring of 1980, I was a senior in high school. As a generally good student, I took a number of college prep courses and one of them was Term Paper Writing. The class, as the name implies, was designed to teach us how to write term papers. We were taught how to create the theme and lay out the body of the writing. We also learned the mechanics of footnotes and bibliographies. Ultimately, at the end of the semester, the bulk of the grade relied upon a successfully completed and turned-in paper. Ten pages. Double-spaced. Typed.

Typed.

I had two major problems with that last requirement. First, I had no idea how to type. This was long before the days when babies were given keyboards to play with in their cribs. In those days, computers filled entire rooms. A laptop was where you put your dinner plate if you didn't have a TV tray. I had never learned anything about the layout of a typewriter. (Typewriter? What's a typewriter?) The second major problem was that I had no typewriter.

Oh, and did I mention that I was a notorious procrastinator? Had I not mentioned that? I suppose I had put it off. It's still an issue, one that I'll eventually get around to dealing with.

The days ticked by and I found myself at 3 PM on the afternoon of the day before the paper was due. I still had no real concept of how to get the paper typed. That was when I came up with a brilliant idea. Desperation is sometimes the breeding ground for creativity. I would go down to the church building and ask if I could use the church's typewriter. Truly, it was my only hope. Either I typed that paper on that typewriter, or I flunked the class—which would have been the only F I had ever received in any class in my entire school career. So, I gathered up my materials, jumped in my dad's 1968 Chevy Nova, and drove to the church building.

"Hi Delores," I said as I entered her tiny office off one end of the big room that we called the old auditorium. Delores was the church secretary or administrator in today's terms. "Can I use the typewriter?" I looked over her shoulder and scanned the huge device with a little trepidation in my heart. It was gray and about as big as a Volkswagen. A power cord snaked out of the side and there was a small, silver ball that jumped with each keystroke.

"Hi Mike," she said as she looked over at me and smiled. It was a genuine smile. Delores was and is a kind person. "Do you know how to type?" She sent a dart into the heart of my plan.

"Umm, well…"

"Have you ever used an electric typewriter before?" she piled on. As her list of questions increased, my hope of surviving my class dwindled. I don't think I mentioned that I'd never used *any* kind of typewriter before—manual or electric.

"No, but I figured I could figure it out." I was a bright kid. I figured stuff out all the time.

"What do you need to type?" She was poking the wound, now.

"I have to type up a ten-page term paper for tomorrow," I admitted. "It has to be typed and this is the only typewriter that I have any access to." I don't recall the exact words, but I was probably about ready to beg. I know panic was setting in.

By now, it was probably 4 PM. Time was ticking away. She would be closing up shop and heading home no later than 5 PM. My paper was due in less than twenty four hours. I had come to her office out of the blue with no warning whatsoever. She looked into the face of the panic-stricken, 18 year old, high school kid who knew that his life was about to end, and she had pity on him.

"I'll type it for you."

I was shocked but incredibly relieved. Hope surged into my heart.

For the next five or six hours, late into the evening, she helped me get that paper typed. We had to get the spacing right and add the footnotes and do the bibliography. There were errors and corrections. White Out. Lots of White Out. (Google it.) Paper went into the machine and paper came out. A few pages were wadded up and thrown in the trash can. I think it was after 10 PM that night when it was all done, but I walked away with a completed paper to turn in the next morning.

Delores has held a special spot in my heart ever since. If it took that long to do, and she was familiar with the machine and knew how to type, then I would have NEVER been able to complete that paper—it would have been impossible for me. I could have pulled an all-nighter in a desperate display of hunting and pecking and still walked out in the early morning light of dawn with no term paper to turn in.

Delores washed my feet.

It wasn't pleasant. It wasn't what was in her plan for that night. It wasn't something anyone would look forward to doing. Still, she volunteered. Her heart went out to me, and she loved me. It would have been so easy to just say no. After all, I was just a high school kid and I didn't even know how to turn on the machine, let alone type on it. She could have just explained that the machine was too expensive for her to risk letting me do what I was asking. She could have sent me on my way—to my impending doom. She could have said that she had plans that evening. She could have done all of that and been completely justified. My predicament was my own fault. I had made my own mess.

It is what we do, you know. We make messes in our lives, and sometimes we need help cleaning them up. There are exceptions (babies born with addiction, child abuse, for example), but in general, alcoholism and drug addiction begin with personal choices—a bad one, or a series of bad ones—that end with a mess. What about destroyed relationships and broken marriages? Husbands and wives choose to cheat. They make a mess of their family. Look around, there are lots of other examples of messes. There are as many different kinds of personal messes as there are different people.

People often make messes of their own lives, and those of us who pretend to "have it together" tend to look down on them, ignoring our own messes, and turn the other way. We turn up our noses and close our eyes. We are often unwilling to sacrifice our time and energy to help because they "are getting what they deserve." After all, they are lying in the bed that they made.

Delores, on the other hand, chose to sacrifice her time and whatever else she was planning to do in order to give me some hope. She saw that I had a burden that I could not bear on my own, so she picked it up and put it on her own shoulders—thus fulfilling the law of Christ—she loved me by meeting the need that I could not fully meet on my own.

The next time you are confronted with someone who has made a mess of things, wash their feet. Get your hands down there in the grime and give them some hope. Bear their burden. Help them get up on their feet again. Maybe by stepping into that mess you can change the trajectory of a life.

Therefore, as we have opportunity, let us do good to all people, especially to those who belong to the family of believers. Galatians 6:10 (NIV)

Discussion Questions

1. Have you ever found yourself in the midst of a problem that you could not handle on your own? Please share.
2. Share about a time when someone went out of their way to help you.
3. How does it make you feel when someone sacrifices to help you in your time of need?
4. Have you ever had someone refuse to help you when you really needed it? How did that feel?
5. Explain how carrying someone else's burden fulfills the law of Christ.

Challenge

This week, look for an opportunity to go out of your way, to sacrifice personal plans, time, or resources, to help someone in need.

Six

Jimmy

Bumblebees and
Forgiveness

"You have heard that it was said, 'Love your neighbor and hate your enemy.' But I tell you, love your enemies and pray for those who persecute you, that you may be children of your Father in heaven." Jesus in Matthew 5:43-45 (NIV)

"For if you forgive other people when they sin against you, your heavenly Father will also forgive you. But if you do not forgive others their sins, your Father will not forgive your sins." Jesus in Matthew 6:14-15 (NIV)

Above all, love each other deeply, because love covers a multitude of sins. I Peter 4:8 (NIV)

When they came to the place called the Skull, they crucified him there, along with the criminals—one on his right, the other on his left.

Jesus said, "Father, forgive them, for they do not know what they are doing." Luke 23:33-34 (NIV)

Back in 1982 or 1983, I remember sitting in a small devotional. It was just four or five guys. The guy leading it was a couple of years older than me and an architect student at Ball State University. I was fresh out of two years of Bible College with my two semesters of ancient (*Koine*) Greek, the language that was used in the writing of most of the New Testament. I don't recall who else was there and I don't recall the main topic of the devo. All I really remember is the disrespect I felt. It made me hurt; it made me mad. There may have been steam coming out of my ears.

In the midst of his message, the young man made the comment that there were three ancient Greek words that are commonly translated into the English word "love." Having just completed two whole semesters of Greek, which is about enough to help me work through a word study if I have the right reference books, I corrected him in front of the group. "Uh, actually, there are four." The guy glared at me.

Let's just say that it didn't end well. He rejected my friendly correction and rejected what I thought was my obviously superior biblical training. I'm not exaggerating to say that I was crushed inside. I'm not joking either. I really was deeply hurt and embarrassed. Not to mention, angry.

So, how many ancient Greek words are commonly translated into the one English word "love?" Frankly, I've matured enough to admit that

I really don't know. My college Greek professor said four, but I truly haven't done an exhaustive study. What I find intriguing as I look back on this story is the oxymoronic nature of that whole situation. Think about it. Here he was discussing love. There I was trying to tell him about the words translated as love. Neither of us reflected love toward one another.

Do you ever wonder why we can remember slights so vividly even across the decades, but it is often quite difficult to remember the nice things that people do for us? These little daggers dig into us, drive wedges into our relationships, and often weasel their way into our self-esteem. We begin to build walls of grudges laid on the foundation of repeated hurts; hurts that are real. Resentment becomes our primary friend. It moves into our mentality and takes up residence. Then, we look back across the days, weeks, months, years, or decades—maybe across a lifetime—and that old pain still controls us. We cannot think of that person without getting angry, maybe even furious.

If I think about that Ball State student's slight from over 35 years ago too long, I would still risk a home invasion by my old nemesis the grudge. Even now. Even me. Even after I can logically understand that I had embarrassed him in front of the other guys. I started it. I was also at fault. Grudges are insidious little dudes.

The story of Jimmy goes back even further— forty plus years. I was in 8th grade. I can still recall the day that Jimmy walked into my math class. I had remembered him from third grade, but he had moved away, and I really hadn't seen him for a long, long time. I remembered him being sort of a bully in elementary school; someone that could quickly get angry and be eager to fight. Still, since I have a naturally trusting nature and I tend to give people the benefit of the doubt, I was happy to see him again. That didn't last very long.

The teacher, for some reason that I still cannot fathom, moved me up from the rear of the class and positioned me right next to Jimmy. I don't think we had finished the first day before he began to terrorize me. Insults, taunts, and jokes at my expense. Somewhere along the line, over the course of the next few days, he began to pester me with a little synthetic bumblebee on a rubber band. He would flick me with it, over and over and over again. His bullying wasn't confined to the math class, but that was where it was the most intense and I couldn't escape it. I could avoid him in the hallways, but in class, I had to sit and pretend I was paying attention despite the little flicks I felt on my ear, my neck, and the side of my face.

At that point in my life, I was a coward. I could have likely saved us both a great deal of pain if I'd just stood my ground and defended myself, but frankly, he scared me. So, I suffered through it—for weeks. As I recall, I could not wait for the school year to end so that I could get away from Jimmy. Frankly, on the inside I was in turmoil. I dreaded getting up in the morning and going to school and the closer the time came for math class, the more intense my inner turmoil became. The trauma was real.

Eventually, though, it ended—both the school year and the bullying. Let me stop for a moment here and say something to anyone who is currently stuck in a situation where they are enduring the intensity of being bullied. I'd like to share two thoughts with you. First, please don't be afraid to get some help. Find someone outside the situation and share with them what is happening. Let them help you. Second, it will change. The situation will not remain the way it is forever. You will emerge on the other side. Don't give in to the temptation to despair.

The school bell rang at the end of the last class on the last day of my eighth-grade school year, and I was free from Jimmy—everywhere but in my mind. The grudge named Jimmy had moved into my memory bank and into my heart. It turned on the tv, got a cold drink, and reclined in its own Lazyboy chair. I think it even had its own bedroom.

The years went by and I grew up, went to college, got married, got a career, and had kids. Still, from time to time, THE GRUDGE would pop back to the front of my mind. The pain. The embarrassment. The anger. The resentment. Many times, I would sit and stew about it, wishing that I had just turned around and punched him square in the mouth. I knew that as a Christian I should forgive, but the grudge wouldn't budge. He had grown comfortable living in my heart. Intellectually, I forgave Jimmy over and over again, but on a deeper level, I couldn't let go of all the pain he had caused me. You see, that pain was real. It was legitimate. It was traumatic. It cannot just be erased from the chalkboard of the mind.

Three decades later, I was in my mid-forties—a grown man with a successful career and a great family. I had lots of friends and was well-respected. I was back in my hometown for business and had decided to hit one of my favorite places for lunch. I grabbed my food, got my drink, and sat down. I liked to look around at the folks in the restaurant, thinking that maybe I'd see someone I knew. Usually I didn't recognize anyone, but I was always hopeful that I'd run into an old friend. On this day, I did see a familiar face on the guy at the next table. He was facing the opposite direction, so we could see each other, and we were close enough to talk. I couldn't place him.

He acknowledged me. His face is very familiar. Still, I can't place it.

"Hi," I said. "You look very familiar."

He smiled a friendly smile. "I'm Jimmy."

The grudge popped to attention. An alarm went off. Lights began to flash. A familiar hurt coupled with simmering anger arose inside my heart. Somehow, I managed to hold it all inside.

We talked for a while and I held it together. He explained that he worked nearby and was on his lunch break. He had been through some tough times in his life. He'd been married and divorced. There had been many mistakes and lots of pain. He shared some of his life's struggles with me—sort of like we had been old friends.

"You know," I said, "you were pretty rough on me back in school." I wasn't angry when I said that, it just seemed to be the right thing to say at that point in the conversation. My heart was softening toward him, but the grudge had to be heard.

Jimmy looked over at me, made eye contact, and said: "I'm really sorry about that." You see, he had found faith in his life and he was trying to make all the changes he needed to get on the best track. I could see the sincerity in his eyes.

As I looked back at him, compassion flooded my mind, and all my pain washed away. The grudge moved out. Or, rather, I was finally able to kick it out. All I could feel was compassion for him. I haven't seen him since, but I wish him well. I hope he has stayed true to his new faith, and that his life is truly changed and renewed. For me, though, those few words he said that day completely reversed the pain he had created all those years before. I was finally able to fully forgive. My compassion (*agape* love) overruled my bitterness as my heart went out to him. As I allowed love to take control, it obliterated the sin that had hurt me so deeply.

Isn't that what Jesus did? In one of the most heart-wrenching, yet personally challenging passages of scripture, Jesus forgave the very people who were crucifying him—while they were in the midst of performing the crucifixion—while they were in the very act. ***"Father, forgive them, for they do not know what they are doing."*** His compassion, his love, overcame the pain and rejection and obliterated the sin they were committing against him, as they were doing it.

Isn't that a challenge for us? I know it's a challenge for me. It took three decades for me to forgive Jimmy, yet Jesus forgave the crucifiers while they were still crucifying him. The key is love. Once love takes the wheel, we can do these difficult things. Remember this passage from the beginning of this chapter?

Above all, love each other deeply, because love covers a multitude of sins. I Peter 4:8 (NIV)

Once we allow compassion to fill our hearts— even toward those who hurt us—we can forgive. We have to. Love and grudges cannot live in the same house.

Discussion

1. Is it easier for you to remember old hurts or old blessings? Why do you think that is?
2. Can you share about an old grudge that you've struggled to deal with?
3. How can compassion overcome grudges in our lives?
4. Why can't love and grudges coexist?
5. Do you find Christ's willingness to immediately forgive his crucifiers personally challenging?

Challenge

Try to track down someone for whom you carry a grudge and attempt to heal the wound through compassion.

Seven

The Cart Kid

"It's More Fun to Forgive"

Love... ...it is not easily angered,... 1 Corinthians 13:5 (NIV)

Refrain from anger and turn from wrath; do not fret—it leads only to evil. Psalm 37:8 (NIV)

My dear brothers and sisters, take note of this: Everyone should be quick to listen, slow to speak, and slow to become angry, because human anger does not produce the righteousness that God desires. James 1:19-20 (NIV)

I think I got the little piece of paper with the joke on it out of a bubble gum wrapper. I remember where I was. I was sitting in the parking lot of Wise Supermarket on East Memorial Drive in Muncie, Indiana as I read the joke. I was just a kid, so this was decades ago. I don't know who made it up, but this is how it went: *"Do you know why matches make such bad friends? It's because they're such hotheads!"*

I don't know why that simple joke has stuck with me over the years. After all, hundreds of thousands of other things passed through my adolescent mind that didn't stick around. Still, that silly joke remains. Perhaps it stuck because there really is a message behind the humor. Frankly, if you cannot control your tendency to get angry, you won't have very many friends.

I've seen it. I've been the recipient of it. Then again, I've done it.

I was riding in the car with someone once when the fellow got angry because the person in front of him was driving too slowly. He sped up on the other car's rear, then suddenly swerved around it only to slam on his breaks right in front of the person. It scared the tar out of me.

Another time, I had a guy chase me down in downtown Indianapolis. I didn't know he was chasing me. I was just driving from my workplace to my wife's workplace to pick her up. Suddenly, while I'm stopped at a light, a guy jumps out of the car behind me and rushes to my window. Luckily, it was only cracked and not wide open. "Don't 'mess' with me," he yelled more than once. He used a more colorful word than 'mess.' I have no idea what I did to make him angry. Maybe I inadvertently cut him off. Anyway, I just looked at him, probably with a shocked look on my face, and said, "okay." Then he stormed back to his car and we both drove off.

I'm not innocent of road rage either. Many years

ago, not long after we had moved back to Indiana from South Carolina, I needed to pick my wife up from her office in one of the downtown Indianapolis towers. For some reason, I had to loop back out of the drop off/pick up area and come around again. As I pulled out, I had it in my head that the street was a one way going to my left. The first two lanes looked open, so I pulled into the roadway. It was then that I realized that it wasn't a one-way street and I was blocking the westbound lanes. A line of traffic going the direction I needed to go was backed up from the light directly in front of me, so I began to look for a way to quickly merge in and get out of the way. I needed someone to let me cut in. As I scanned the faces of the people in the other cars, hoping for a little help, one guy looked me in the eye, wagged his finger at me, and shook his head. He was giving me a belligerent no.

My anger exploded!

Couldn't he see that I was just trying to get out of the way? Couldn't he understand the urgent anxiety I was feeling from facing the wrong way into oncoming traffic? Well, of course not. He couldn't read my mind. From his perspective, I was just trying to force my way in front of him instead of waiting my turn. I can reason that out now, but in the heat of the moment, I was burning the bright hot flame of indignation.

As he passed by, the guy behind him let me in. I got right up behind the man with the wagging finger and followed him for several blocks to make sure he understood just how much he had mistreated me. I don't know what I would have done if he had stopped and gotten out of his car, but I was in the red zone and steam was coming out of my ears. By the way, did I mention that it was Christmas Eve? Merry Christmas, y'all.

Traffic and road rage are just one set of circumstances where our anger surges. It can happen almost anywhere. Maybe you've been standing in a long check-out lane for a while when the lane next to you opens up. With blatant disregard for how long you've been waiting, however, some dude, who hasn't even been in line yet, steps up to the front. Maybe you're waiting at a service counter and someone gets served before you. Maybe you're driving to the hoop and the defender gives you a hard foul, knocking you to the floor. Maybe your daughter is up to bat in her third-grade softball game and she gets called out on a bogus third strike by an adolescent umpire. The surge of anger can come out of nowhere at almost any given moment.

Where does anger show up in your life? I must admit that it shows up in mine.

It was just a few weeks prior to this writing that I was sitting in my wife's Subaru Forester in the Walmart parking lot in Franklin, Indiana. My 92-year old mother-in-law was in the front passenger seat and I was behind the wheel. We were waiting for my wife to come out with the few groceries that her mother would need for the coming week. As we were making small talk, I attempted to whistle a short little tune. I told her that I was trying to remember the tune from the Andy Griffith show, but I thought I was whistling the Gomer Pyle theme instead. Then, I asked her if she could whistle. To my surprise, she puckered up and did it. She whistled. I got a kick out of it. It was funny and it was fun. It was a nice moment. We were smiling at one another.

Suddenly, we were rocked out of our nice moment when something banged into the front of the Subaru. I looked up to see a whole line of carts passing by. It was literally about a thirty-foot string of carts. There was a cart guy leading the way and a machine driving the train from the rear. I raised my hands and glared at the kid leading the way.

"Sorry," he said as he kept going.

The string kept moving and then it banged into my bumper again.

"Hey," I said through the window and raised my arms in protest.

"Sorry," he said again as the train kept moving.

As I watched in disbelief, the machine driving the train rammed into the front driver's side corner of our vehicle.

"Sorry," he said one more time as he kept moving the long line of carts through the parking lot.

That third time took the cake. I jumped out of the car, leaving my elderly mother-in-law in an anxious state, and yelled at the young man as I rushed around to look at the damage. I knew there had to be damage because the entire vehicle had rocked violently. Sure enough, the plastic was mangled and deformed where the machine had slammed into it.

"Hey!" I yelled. "You damaged my car?"

"Sorry," he called back, now from an aisle over.

"Sorry isn't going to cut it!" I replied. "You bungled up the bumper!"

"Sorry," he said one more time. He seemed so callous and unconcerned.

I couldn't believe that he didn't stop and redirect when he first hit my car. I couldn't believe that he didn't stop and come back to see what he had done. I couldn't believe he just kept walking away. His response of "sorry" seemed so disconnected and disregarding of what had actually occurred. He really had damaged my wife's car. I was fuming and I knew I had to do something. It was at that moment that my wife returned.

"What's going on?" she asked.

"That guy bungled up our bumper with his cart machine," I explained. "He hit us like three times and just kept going. Look at that!" I pointed out the damage and took a picture with my phone.

"What are you going to do?" she asked.

"I guess I need to go find a manager," I said and then stormed off toward the store.

As I approached the store, I saw the cart kid over to the right of the door where the carts get lined up. He was walking toward the building and talking to someone that was around the corner and out of my line of sight. I angled toward him. I was going to confront him directly and then go find his manager. When I got closer, I could hear his voice.

"I really felt bad," he said.

I rounded the corner and made my final approach. "Where's your manager?" I demanded.

"That's the guy," he told the people that I could

now see to my left, a man and a woman. They jumped in to speak on his behalf.

"We're going to get the manager," the woman said.

"It was the first time for him driving that many carts," the man stated.

"Look," I said, "I really don't want anything, but he bungled up the bumper of my car."

I looked at the young man. "You should have stopped. You should have come back."

"I was going to come back. I was just trying to get the carts out of the parking lot first."

It was at about that moment that I realized something key to the situation. The cart kid was a special needs person. It really was an accident. He really was sorry. He was just trying to do his job.

"I really am sorry," he said as he stuck out his hand to me.

The woman again said: "We're going to get the manager right now."

All of the anger melted out of my heart. I took his hand and shook it. "You're really sorry?" I asked.

"I really am," he answered.

"Then, I think we'll just let it go," I told him. "The car's got some age on it anyway." Then, I smiled at him and added: "Maybe next time, how about you make it a few less carts?"

I smiled. He smiled. His two coworkers looked like they'd just won the lottery. Huge smiles. All of the fear, anxiety, and potential conflict was replaced with joy, relief, and a sense of peace. My bumper was still a bit mangled, but I headed back to my slightly less pristine Forester feeling pretty doggone good.

I jumped back behind the wheel of the Subaru and started it up. My mother-in-law was worried. "What's going to happen?" she asked.

"Nothing," I said. "I forgave him." Then, I added out of the joy in my heart: "Besides, it's a whole lot more fun to forgive than it is to be angry."

Just like with grudges, compassion cannot coexist with anger. If you allow love to be your driving influence, then the resulting compassion will overrule the anger that surges to the surface.

Discussion Questions

1. Share about a time when you were very angry. Describe how it made you feel.
2. Have you ever had someone misinterpret your words or intentions and respond in anger? How did you feel?
3. Have you ever experienced a time when you allowed compassion to overrule your anger?
4. What are some ways that anger can lead to hurtful consequences?
5. How can compassion change the situation and bring about positive consequences?

Challenge

Over the next week, any time that you feel anger surging to the surface of your heart, challenge yourself to find a way to approach the situation with compassion.

MICHAEL DECAMP

Eight

Ernest

Hand-me-downs to the Rescue

"Then the King will say to those on his right, 'Come, you who are blessed by my Father; take your inheritance, the kingdom prepared for you since the creation of the world. For I was hungry and you gave me something to eat, I was thirsty and you gave me something to drink, I was a stranger and you invited me in, I needed clothes and you clothed me, I was sick and you looked after me, I was in prison and you came to visit me.'

"Then the righteous will answer him, 'Lord, when did we see you hungry and feed you, or thirsty and give you something to drink? When did we see you a stranger and invite you in, or needing clothes and clothe you? When did we see you sick or in prison and go to visit you?'

"The King will reply, 'Truly I tell you, whatever you did for one of the least of these brothers and sisters of mine, you did for me.'"
Matthew 25:34-40 (NIV)

Jesus' story about the sheep and the goats ought to cause those of us in the modern church to pause. Perhaps, we should get a little uncomfortable in our pews. We are so caught up in being right. Doctrine is so important to us. Our brand of Christianity (pick any of them) is the one that has the best handle on the truth, right? This church condemns that church. Brother rejects brother over technical matters of doctrine. Sister rejects sister over similar issues. Baptism. Music. Contemporary versus Traditional. This person's role versus that person's role. The Holy Spirit. You name it. We fight, we fuss, and we squabble. The problem is that none of that is of any concern in Matthew 25. Not a single point of doctrine is taken into account. I'm not saying that doctrine isn't important, or that it doesn't have its place. However, I am saying that we have misplaced its priority. This story makes loving others the priority.

Jesus drives home the point that what it all comes down to is how well we take care of one another's needs. Did we love one another in tangible ways that made a difference? Were our convictions strong enough to drive us to action?

I didn't have many hand-me-downs as a child. My closest sibling turned sixteen about two weeks prior to my birth. In fact, there was such a gap in our ages that I really spent my childhood living as if

I were an only child. Each fall, about a week before school would start, my mother would take me shopping for school clothes. It was important to her that I have nice clothes for school, dress clothes. In her mind, that meant a great deal of polyester.

I was a freshman in high school before I could join the rest of my teenage peers in wearing denim to class. Even then, I had to beg my mother to let me wear my jeans and Converse basketball shoes instead of plastic slacks and brown faux leather dress boots. Eventually, she relented, and I was finally allowed to dress to blend in.

I don't resent Mom's obsession with dressing me as nice as she could for school. In her day, boys who wore jeans to school were the poorest kids, the ones who were simply unable to wear anything better and they were often the targets of derision. She wanted better for me. However, society had shifted, and jeans had become commonplace. School had gone casual. Dress clothes made me a target, but she was oblivious. She didn't know any better.

So, the clothes that I got were normally new when I got them. Not that I had expensive stuff. Quite the opposite. My wardrobe came from Sears, JC Penney, or a local bargain clothing store. Though new, my clothes were modest. Designer clothes were never hanging in my closet. No, my clothes were nothing special; they just weren't stuff that used to be someone else's stuff.

In August of 1986, my wife and I moved to Columbia, South Carolina so that I could take a position as a ministry intern. After high school, I had attended Williamstown Bible College in West Virginia and I had maintained my desire and plan to work in the ministry into our early marriage. My chance finally came that year. A friend of mine had taken on the lead minister position at a church in Columbia, and I received the opportunity to move there to serve and train. Nancy and I pulled up stakes, packed a small U-Haul truck, and headed south.

Before we left, we were both working regular, entry-level jobs. We were newlyweds with no kids, but with double incomes, living in a very inexpensive one and a half bedroom rented house. After we moved, we were a single-income couple living in a more expensive apartment that was smack dab in the middle of city with a higher cost of living. We were living on Nancy's income as the church secretary. My income was tiny. I had a meager (but much appreciated) amount of monthly support from a few friends, and I got a $100 per month stipend to manage the janitorial staff of the church. To say we had a tight budget is to underestimate how taut our shoestring funds were in the reality of our ministry world. Money was so scarce that we celebrated our second anniversary in a borrowed van, camping on a state park beach. However, despite how short of funds we were, it always seemed that God would come through. More than once, I had almost reached a point of desperation when a check would show up in the mail. That happened over and over again.

One event during that year in South Carolina put us into a genuine bind. We lived on the second floor of an apartment building. There were eight units in our breezeway and we all shared a common laundry room on the ground level. There were two washers and two dryers available. There was no set schedule, but we all cooperated. Generally, you loaded up your clothes for a wash then left them. A few minutes later, you'd come back and switch them to the dryer. No conflicts, no issues.

One evening, my wife loaded up my clothes. I didn't have much, so it wasn't a big deal. Basically, all of my clothes were in two groups: white clothes and everything else. She had put my "everything else" through the wash and into the dryer, and had gone back upstairs to wait for them to dry. When I went down to retrieve them, they were gone.

Nearly every decent pair of pants and every decent shirt I had was history. Someone had stolen my clothes right out of the dryer. I didn't have much more than the clothes I was wearing, and no money to get anything new. I found myself in sudden real need. The shoestring holding our finances together had been ripped out of the shoe. Frankly, I was completely at a loss for what to do. I had virtually no clothes and literally no money to get any clothes.

The following Sunday word had gotten around about my situation. I've never been very good at keeping my business to myself and I had told a few people what had happened. I still wasn't sure what to do. I was probably planning to see if I could get some money from my parents since all of the money in our bank account was already spoken for. That was when Ernest showed up.

Ernest was about my size and about my age. He and I knew each other, but I wouldn't say we were close. While we were in the same church, the ministries of that congregation were organized by geography into separate regions, and he was in another region. Still, I remember him being a good-natured guy and easy to be around. I liked him.

Apparently someone had shared my predicament with him because he walked up to me that following Sunday morning and handed me a large, paper sack—full to the top. At first, I didn't know what it was, but when I looked inside, I found multiple pairs of pants and dress shirts—all my size. He had gone to his closet and pulled a boatload of his own clothes out so that I could have my need met. I will also say that these were not his dregs. They may have been used, but they were in good shape. They were nice. They not only met my immediate need, but were useful to me for a good two or three years following.

By that simple gesture, Ernest lifted me out of a financial crisis and gave me room to breathe. I'm still not sure what I would have done, but that is a moot point. He changed the trajectory of the situation by handing me a paper bag full of *agape* love.

As of this writing, that was thirty-one years ago, and I have not forgotten his act of kindness that made such a difference to me in my time of need. Many people said things to me during that time: "Oh, I'm so sorry!" "That's terrible!" "Did they catch them?" I don't recall anything specific about those conversations and don't even recall the faces of the people who shared those sentiments. They made no lasting impact on my life. However, I remember Ernest. He made a difference to me. He clothed me; he loved me. I believe he's got a seat reserved on the right side of that great, final assembly.

Discussion Questions

1. When you boil it all down, what is the bottom line of Jesus' story of the sheep and the goats? Read the full passage again. Matthew 25:31-46
2. Why do we put so much energy into having the right doctrine and so little energy into meeting needs?
3. Share about a time when someone truly met a need in your life.
4. Thinking about the poor, the hungry, the sick, the imprisoned, what are specific needs that you see in your community?
5. What role does fear play in meeting needs? How can you overcome it?

Challenge

Open your eyes to the needs around you this week. Identify a need that you can meet in someone else's life by giving them something that you already have. Sacrifice a possession.

Nine

Angela

The Great Soda Can Debacle

A gentle answer turns away wrath, but a harsh word stirs up anger. Proverbs 15:1 (NIV)
Fathers, do not embitter your children, or they will become discouraged. Colossians 3:21 (NIV)
Love is patient, love is kind. 1 Corinthians 13:4 (NIV)

My dad was basically a good man. I shared in the introduction about how he introduced me to the concept of loving God—a gift for which I will always be thankful. Still, he had one significant fault. He had a temper. There were many times that I was hurt by his words as I was growing up, but this chapter isn't about his mistakes. It is about mine. You see, I have a temper, too.

Before I get to the heart of the story, let me just share this: I am basically an insecure, hyper-sensitive person. That was especially true when I was young and I have toughened up as I've aged, but even today, that old insecurity can sneak up and bite me when I'm least expecting it. I doubt I was always insecure, but I'm sure I was always very sensitive.

I don't really mind the sensitivity. It promotes empathy. I can feel what others are feeling. I can sense pain in another's words. It makes me compassionate. It also makes me cry at movies, but we won't go there.

The problem evolves when you take a sensitive person and subject them to ridicule, teasing, or other kinds of bullying. Frankly, that was my youth from the time I started school. Sometimes it was as simple as teases about my weight. Words that many people would brush aside, a sensitive person will take to heart. Other times, it was taunts and threats. Either way, the end result was that I added insecurity to my list of character flaws.

Maturity did help alleviate the intensity of the bullying that I faced in school. I think I grew about six inches between eighth and ninth grades, so most of the abusers backed off—not all, but most. Still, the insecurity was already imbedded.

Over the years, I've had various influences that have helped me to grow in my character. Those influences have, over time, decreased the insecurity to minimal levels, but I doubt it will ever be completely wiped away, at least not in this lifetime. The first influence to help me change was my high school youth group and the youth minister who saw something in me that made him think I could be a leader. The second were the girls that found me "date-able." The third is the woman who would become (and is) my wife. Also, in the mix is the time I spent in the paint under the basket in church-league basketball, where I laid the smack down on anyone who was brave enough to come into the paint. Finally, there is my career in sales that has put me in front of all sorts of people and forced me to push through any fear that I might have in order to speak publicly.

That's all wonderful, but as I said, it still, sometimes, sneaks up and bites me. And, before you begin to feel sympathy for my character flaws, please understand that whatever may have caused my personal insecurities, it is no excuse for treating others with anything less than kindness and patience. Love demands that I overcome my selfish insecurity in order to embrace my ability and responsibility to build others up.

Now, for the story of "Angela and the Great Soda Can Debacle."

Parenting is one of those jobs that you mostly learn by doing. Sure, there are great books out there. If you are lucky, you may find some great examples of other parents who seem to have it all locked up. The problem is that every child is different and you don't get any real practice until you're in the middle of the championship game. You can't know how you will handle the screaming baby, the ink marks on the new car upholstery, the broken dishes, the sharp little Lego block left on the floor in the dark, or the independent teenager until you are in the midst of the real-life, all-out, high-stakes, more-than-a-game, responsibility of being a parent.

Angela is my oldest daughter. She is blessed with my sensitivity and her mother's bluntness. What she thinks or feels on the inside is often expressed openly on the outside. Ultimately, this is one of her finest traits and I am incredibly proud of her—I think it helps her to express real emotion in her paintings (see angeladecamp.com), but I have not always handled her bluntness in the most appropriate way.

As a man from the tail end of the Baby Boomer generation—right or wrong—I was raised with the expectation that I should be respected as a father and as the leader of my household. You can challenge whether that is an appropriate expectation to have, but regardless, it was the expectation that was ingrained into my understanding of fatherhood. My problem, however, was that I viewed any challenge to what I said or decided through the lens of my personal insecurity. If Angela reacted to me—with the honesty of her inside-out character—I would feel disrespected. It felt like an attack on my value as a father. My insecurity would rear up and kick like a startled horse.

It was late one evening, probably after 11 P.M. My wife and both daughters were in bed. Earlier, I had seen Angela step out into the garage to get a can of soda. We had a mini fridge and a supply of extras in a stash just beside it. The stash was in those long cardboard cartons. I think each carton held twenty-four cans. They were laid on their sides with the ends torn out, which was sort of stupid because then the cans had the tendency to simply roll out of the carton. That is exactly what had happened.

I stepped out there—I don't recall why—and I saw a mess. Multiple soda cans had rolled out of the cartons and had fallen on the concrete floor. A few had broken open and sugary soda had spurted out. My temper rose up and took control. Since Angela had been the last one out there, I was determined that she be the one to clean it up—despite the fact that she was already in bed for the night, asleep. She was fourteen.

I marched angrily up the stairs to her bedroom and knocked loudly on her door. She came groggily over, opened the door, and looked out at me. The exchange went something like this:

Me: "Come with me!"

Angela: "Why?"

Me: "There is soda all over the garage floor and you were the last one to get one. You're going to clean it up!"

Angela: "Can't I do it tomorrow? I'm tired. I was asleep."

Me: "No! You are going to clean it up now! Right now!"

In my anger, I woke up my wife—which is no easy task—and I woke up my younger daughter. Our exchange continued down the stairs and out into the garage. Believe it or not, I got even more angry and even more loud. Angela voiced her issue with how I was treating her, and that is when it happened. My insecurity took over. I snapped. I don't really recall the words, but I was determined that she would respect me—she would obey me—I was her father and she would do as I said. I was not about to allow any disrespect to go unanswered. I pretty much unloaded on her.

The funny thing about respect is that when you demand it, when you try to force it, that effort tends to have the opposite effect.

It was close to midnight. Our house was located on a dark country road. The garage door was wide open. Angela was in her pajamas. She wasn't wearing shoes. I was angrily yelling at her. Finally, she had enough and turned away, rushing out into the dark, down the driveway, and down the road—barefooted.

I let her go and walked into the house, still fuming. My wife met me just inside.

"She's gone," I said.

"What do you mean 'she's gone'?" Nancy responded.

"She took off out the door and down the road," I explained.

Nancy looked me square in the eyes and in a voice I will not soon forget, said: "YOU WILL FIND MY DAUGTHER RIGHT NOW!"

That shocked me back to reality, so I turned around and went after Angela. As it turns out, she was on her way back anyway. She had decided that being barefoot on the county road in the middle of the night was not a good idea. I met her in the driveway and we both went back inside.

I don't remember who cleaned up the sodas, but I do remember the trauma of the event. For a while,

I felt justified. After all, she was my child and she needed to obey me. Further, she needed to respect my authority in her life. However, as I have aged and continued to mature, I see that I treated her harshly. I allowed my anger and especially my insecurity to drive how I dealt with what, in the grand scheme of things, was really a minor situation. I turned a mole hill into a mountain, and hurt people—not just Angela, but also my wife and my younger daughter. It is an event that we all remember to this day.

Instead of assuming the best, I had assumed the worst: she was the last one there, so she must have caused the mess. Well, maybe so, but also maybe not. Perhaps, the vibrations of someone climbing the household stairs had caused the cans to break free and roll onto the floor. The problem was that I assumed the worst. Love always trusts, but I had done the opposite.

Instead of treating her with kindness, I confronted her with harshness. The whole event would have turned out differently if I had denied myself and just cleaned up the mess. I could have discussed it with the whole family the next day, and explained that we needed to change how we stocked the sodas. Eventually, I did apologize to Angela. In fact, we discussed the event in detail as I prepared this chapter and she helped me reconstruct some of the details. We've grown quite close despite my mistakes.

I don't know how the sodas got all over the floor, but I know that it was me that caused the real mess by not truly loving my daughter the way that

God intended. I wasn't patient. I wasn't kind. I was self-seeking. I didn't trust.

Sometimes, it seems that those we care about the most are the ones that we treat the worst. I would have never spoken to or treated an employee or a co-worker that way. Maybe it's because our inherent insecurities are the most vulnerable to those to whom we are the closest. Family can push our buttons, often without intending to, and we feel free to blow our lids. Can we admit, though, that doing that just doesn't work? It never ends well. We don't end up with respect. We just damage or break the relationships with those that we emotionally love the most.

Discussion Questions

1. Share about a time when you lost your temper. What was the end result?
2. What is the underlying issue that drives your temper? Insecurity? Fear? Anxiety? Other?
3. Considering the same event, how could you have approached the same situation with kindness and patience?
4. Why is it that the people to whom we are the closest are also the ones to whom we are the most harsh?
5. Do you have any broken relationships that you can trace back to harsh words?

Challenge

Think about someone to whom you have reacted harshly and have hurt. Contact them and humbly apologize without offering any excuses.

Ten

Paul

A Key for the Prodigal

Love...
...it keeps no record of wrongs.
It always trusts... (1 Corinthians 13:5 & 7 NIV)

Have you ever said goodbye to someone without realizing that it really was the last time you would see them for a very long time—maybe forever? I know that when I graduated from high school, I didn't realize that it would take Facebook and the passing of thirty years before I reconnected with so many of the kids that I had gone to class with for years.

In another example, I remember walking out of a church meeting one time. I had been paged for work. This was back when everyone had pagers instead of smart phones. The man conducting the meeting was a friend and one of my former Bible College teachers. I caught his eye as I stood to leave. We acknowledged one another and I nodded. That was 1994. As I write this, it is May 2018 and I still have not seen him since that day. Within a day of that meeting, our church had a huge rift that left me with one group and him with the other. In the last fifteen years, we have spoken and connected on social media. We have no lingering issues, but that was definitely not what I expected to happen as I left that room so many years ago.

Sometimes, life throws curveballs, and sometimes we are simply oblivious to what our choices do to our relationships.

In August of 1986, my wife and I moved from Muncie, Indiana to Columbia, South Carolina, leaving behind my home church. The Fairlawn church in Muncie was where the love for God that my dad had instilled in me had blossomed and grown. It was where I'd matured and grown confident through my involvement in the youth group. It was where I had met my wife. When I left, they were a special and important group of people to me.

After I moved, though, I became enveloped in new groups of people—first in Columbia, and then, later, in Indianapolis. We lived in Columbia for a year before we moved back to Indiana and settled in Indianapolis. The church we were part of in Indianapolis was larger and very active. They dominated much of our time and they had pockets of members spread across central Indiana. We spent about two and half years in Indy, but during that time, we became entrenched in that ministry to the exclusion of many of our previous relationships. I allowed responsibilities, obligations, and the demands of others to drive out my devotion to previous relationships—including my Fairlawn church family.

In 1990, my work moved me back to Muncie. You would think that I would have reconnected to that church family that had meant so much to me in my youth, but that's not what happened. The church in Indy had a pocket of people in Muncie that traveled to Indianapolis for worship. Rather than renew with my original church home, I stayed with the Indy group. I didn't even occasionally visit to see people and maintain the relationships. A couple of times, I asked for our group to be allowed to use their baptistery. Otherwise, I had zero contact—not even to spend time in fellowship. I allowed my involvement in the Indianapolis group to crowd out my love and devotion to that church that had originally changed my life.

Time passed and I moved again, and yet again. Eventually, I ended up back in Indianapolis. Another ten years went by, and I had no contact with my Muncie home church during that entire decade. None. Zip. Zero. They were in my rearview mirror and I had no motivation to do anything about it. Frankly, I was too busy to think about it.

Then my father died, and we had to plan the funeral back in Muncie.

I don't know the traditions in other places, but in Indiana, it is traditional for the family to have a reception following the funeral. My parents had sold their home a few years earlier and had even moved down to live with us in Indianapolis the previous year. My brother and sister both lived in Muncie, but their homes were too small. We had no obvious place for a reception short of renting a facility.

After some thought, I decided that maybe the Fairlawn church would let me rent out their basement, which was their space for group pitch-ins or potluck meals. I thought it might be a good option, if they had someone who could let us in and if it wasn't already booked for something else. I trusted that they would let me rent it, if they could. That was my hope, anyway. Then again, it had been over ten years since I had even visited one of their services. Maybe they would turn me away. They certainly had no obligation to me.

I walked up to the front doors sort of sheepishly. I suppose I felt a little guilty. I might have felt a little like the Prodigal Son returning to a home he didn't deserve. I rang the bell and Paul came to let me in.

He led the way and I followed him up into the same little office where Delores had typed my term paper twenty years earlier. He greeted me warmly, which was what I had hoped and expected, especially when I realized that it would be Paul that I would meet with that day. He sat behind a little desk and I sat beside it.

Paul has that sort of Barnabas quality. He is a true "son of encouragement." He has a certain warmth about him that draws people in. Those kinds of folks are rare, but you know them when you see them. Encouragement tends to exude from their pores.

"How can we help you, Mike?" Paul asked.

With some hesitation, I shared my predicament. "My mom and dad moved to Indy last year," I explained, "but my father has just died. We are planning the funeral and we have no place to have the reception…"

Before I could finish the story, Paul pulled out the middle drawer of his desk. He lifted a key from the tray and handed it to me. It was the key to the building. No questions. No collateral. No forms to fill out. Just love dangling from a little silver ring.

"You're giving me a key to the building?" I said with a question in my voice. I was shocked. "I haven't been here in ten years."

He looked me in the eyes and said, "You're one of us."

I was deeply touched. His trust and warmth toward me nearly overwhelmed me. I may have even teared up a bit. Still, I was heartbroken that I had allowed my devotion to that church family to be ignored for so very long. Something changed in me that day. I learned an important lesson and my heart left that room different than it was before I entered it.

The icing on the cake was the day of the funeral. Not only did they give me access to the building (no charge), but they also provided much of the food, partnering with my Indianapolis church family. Paul, his wife Wanda, and a number of other Fairlawn church members were there, serving my family. I may have ignored them for over ten years, but they never stopped caring for me.

Paul loved me when he handed me that key. He trusted me—love always trusts. He forgave me—love keeps no record of wrongs.

Before typing this, I saw Paul and I mentioned to him that I was going to write this chapter. I told him that it was devoted to him and as I should have expected, he gave all the credit to his wife, Wanda. He explained that if she had not loved him first, he would not have had the character he needed to love me on that day, during my time of need. Love may trust and keep no record of wrongs, but it also pays it forward. When you love someone, that love is compounded; it spills out, and splatters all over other people. You may never know all of the positive side effects that may come as a result.

Discussion Questions

1. Can you think of people that when you parted from them, you didn't realize that you wouldn't see them again?
2. Do you have important relationships that have fallen by the wayside because you've allowed circumstances to drive a wedge between you and them?
3. Can you think of someone who has given you the grace of trust and forgiveness?
4. Is there someone in your life who has changed you by showing you love?
5. If "love always trusts" and "doesn't keep a record of wrongs," how does your life reflect those characteristics?

Challenge

Think of an individual that was important to you but with whom you have fallen out of touch. Take steps to find them and reconnect.

Eleven

Brian

A Superhero and His Sidekick

Two are better than one, because they have a good return for their labor: If either of them falls down, one can help the other up. But pity anyone who falls and has no one to help them up. Also, if two lie down together they will keep warm. But how can one keep warm alone? Though one may be overpowered, two can defend themselves. A cord of three strands is not quickly broken. Ecclesiastes 4:9-12 (NIV)

Carry each other's burdens, and in this way you will fulfill the law of Christ. Galatians 6:2 (NIV)

Some men came carrying a paralyzed man on a mat and tried to take him into the house to lay him before Jesus. When they could not find a way to do this because of the crowd, they went up on the roof and lowered him on his mat through the tiles into the middle of the crowd, right in front of Jesus. Luke 5:18-19 (NIV)

A man was going down from Jerusalem to Jericho, when he was attacked by robbers. They stripped him of his clothes, beat him and went away, leaving him half dead. A priest happened to be going down the same road..., he passed by on the other side. So too, a Levite, when came to the place..., passed by on the other side. But a Samaritan, as he traveled, came where the man was; and when he saw him, he took pity on him. He went to him and bandaged his wounds, pouring oil and wine. Then he put the man on his own donkey, brought him to an inn and took care of him. Luke 10:30-34 (NIV)

This is one chapter where you might say: TMI—too much information. Hang with me, though, because I think the example I'm going to highlight here is one of the most challenging.

Paul says in one of the verse's I've highlighted above that in "carrying each other's burdens" we "fulfill the law of Christ." I've become convinced that the specific law that he is referring to is the law of love—to love one another, just as he has loved us. Still, many of us shy away from jumping into opportunities to provide *agape* love because it requires direct involvement in someone else's mess—getting your hands dirty, so to speak.

It also takes commitment. If you take the leap and involve yourself, then you are committed to seeing it through. There's no halfway. It's all in or you've dropped the ball.

It's easier to look the other way, to ignore the need, to pretend you don't see or hear the call for help. "Someone else will help him," we often tell ourselves. We, like the priest and the Levite, pass by on the other side of the road. It's not my problem.

Back in my late teens and early twenties, I knew some college boys at the Fairlawn church where I attended who took charge of assisting another young man who was also a college student. He had cerebral palsy and was wheelchair bound. This was long before the days when accessibility was mandated by law, and they would need to help him up and down stairs and maneuver him around obstacles. Further, he could not fully accomplish his needs in the bathroom without assistance. I was impressed by the college men who volunteered to help him, but I never jumped in to assist. I passed by on the other side.

It doesn't have to be a long-term issue or even a physical one. It could be that someone just needs someone to talk to, someone to lend an ear. Maybe they only need someone to look them in the eye and actually care. We are afraid of what it will lead to, however, so we pass by on the other side. It could be that a marriage is struggling, and we could provide some guidance and support. Instead, we tend to shy away from the couple until they get their act together—passing by on the other side. Maybe someone has a financial crisis and we can pitch in some cash, but instead we wish them well and point them to the bank—passing by on the other side. It really could be any need that we could help carry, but choose not to help.

Sometimes, though, God doesn't really leave you room to make the choice.

A while back, I was at the church building a little early to prepare for a class. After depositing my materials in the classroom, I ducked into the men's room. I was about to take care of my own need when I heard someone speak from a nearby stall. It was sort of a mumble, so I wasn't sure what had been said.

"What's that?" I replied.

"I need help," said the man.

I recognized the voice. It was an elderly gentleman, a long-time member, and someone who could no longer easily get around.

I had noticed a heavy odor when I'd entered and had hoped to finish my business quickly, but that hope immediately evaporated. I was the only other person in the room and there weren't all that many other people even in the building, yet. This was on me. No passing by on the other side.

I stepped around to the front of the stall with some trepidation and asked him what he needed. He didn't really need to tell me. It was obvious. He had experienced an intestinal issue. Both he and his clothes were in a mess. I am understating the situation. It was really bad. Plus, the odor was nearly overpowering me.

The truth is that I wanted to run the other way. I wanted out of the situation. However, God had put me in a position where I had no choice but to assist.

I couldn't walk away. I couldn't abandon the elderly gentlemen to sit in his own waste until someone with a better heart happened by. That said, I also recognized right away that I couldn't handle this alone. I needed help.

That is when Brian stepped in.

I told the man that I needed to get some help and stepped out into the building lobby to see who I could approach. My friend Brian responded immediately, following me back to the restroom. I explained the predicament along the way. The man was a mess both on his body and his clothes, as well.

When we reentered, this time the odor truly overpowered me. I could no longer control my gag reflex and I was forced to keep exiting. I was ashamed, but it was more than I could handle. Brian, on the other hand, was able to hold it together and took charge. That didn't release me from responsibility, however. I had to see it through. I became Brian's resource for materials. He sent me first for paper towels, and later for some sort of temporary clothing. While I was on my errands, Brian helped the man get cleaned up, and rinsed out his clothing.

Ultimately, the man's clothing was too soiled and was wet from being rinsed out. He couldn't put them back on. Further, I could find nothing useful anywhere else in the building. Brian decided that he would run to his own home to retrieve the man some dry clothes to wear. Since the situation was stable and I had my class to lead, we recruited a third man to stand guard at the bathroom door to

and potential titles. The picture below is one of those designs. I share it in his honor.

This chapter is dedicated to the memory of James Persinger, the elderly gentleman. He passed in 2019, only a short time after giving me the drawings. Thank you, Jim, for your support.

Twelve

Todd

Trash-talking Takes a Toll

Like a maniac shooting flaming arrows of death is one who deceives their neighbor and says, "I was only joking!" Proverbs 26:18-19 (NIV)

Do not let any unwholesome talk come out of your mouths, but only what is helpful for building others up according to their needs, that it may benefit those who listen. Ephesians 4:29 (NIV)

In the first chapter, I shared with you about my tendency to try to be funny—sometimes at someone else's expense. In this chapter, I'm going to revisit that topic, but with a slightly different angle. The point will be similar, but with a different nuance.

Trash-talking is commonplace in the world of professional sports. Players make an art of it. I saw a replay the other day of a legendary NBA game five between the Indiana Pacers and the New York Knicks where Reggie Miller caught fire carrying the Pacers to a victory. In the midst of that flurry of three-pointers, he performed his trademark "choke" sign to Spike Lee. Why? Because Spike had been trash-talking him through the whole series. In the NFL, the trash talk has progressed to the level that they had to institute a taunting penalty to rein it in—to keep it at the verbal level. As fans, we find it funny and exciting if it is our team or player, but infuriating if it is the opposing team or player.

As a young man in my thirties, I played quite a bit of church-league basketball. I didn't have much skill. In fact, I was so bad at basketball as a youth that I was still improving when I hit forty years old. However, the one skill I did have, I used to my advantage: I was a pretty big guy. I would plant myself in the paint, near the basket, on defense and dare anyone to come in there. If they did, and I was still low in fouls, I would make it an experience to remember. I put more than one person on the floor. I wanted them to be thinking about that the next time they drove to the basket.

I remember one game in particular where my shooting guard was consistently being held by his defender. When he told me about it, I said, "I'll take care of it." The next time my guy had the ball, I came out to set a screen. My guy came around me, followed by the offending defender. I put the guy on the floor, stood over him, and said: "If you keep holding him, you'll get more."

Hallelujah! Let's sing some worship songs. It

was a church league after all.

"Well," you might say, "it's just part of the game. You're just getting in their head."

To a point, I don't disagree. Still, sometimes those words or actions are carried off the court. It's important that everyone is on the same page that it's just a game, that everyone is "all good" after the game is over. Generally, my opponents laughed about my antics. They had a name for it: "You got DeCamped!" The funny thing was that my court persona was so very different from my real world persona—easy-going, light-hearted and friendly.

Trash-talking in a game is one thing. Trash-talking in our relationships is another thing altogether. It is something men do all the time. We call one another names, pick at one another's quirks, and laugh at one another's mistakes. Make fun of one another's views. You could say it's a guy thing.

Clint Eastwood directed and starred in a movie a few years ago called Gran Torino. The movie is a dramatic character study of an aging blue-collar white man in Detroit coping with an influx of people into his neighborhood who were very different from him. They were different in race, in age, and in culture. Clint's character was rough and crude. He was a true curmudgeon. In the midst of the cultural conflicts, he befriends a young boy from the differing culture, and in one of the scenes, he is trying to teach him "how men talk to one another." He takes the boy into a local barbershop to teach him the fine points of trash-talking. I can't describe the conversation because the language is inappropriate for this book, but it was a classic scene that truly describes common practice in the interaction of men in all walks of life.

I'm no different. I'm just as prone as the next guy to practice the fine art of friendly trash-talking. Even as I do it, though, I think about my friend Todd—my former friend.

Todd and I were the same age. He was from Ohio and I was from Indiana. As I recall, we met right before our first week of classes at Bible College in Williamstown, West Virginia. Right off, we became friends. We hung together in classes. We studied together. We discussed spiritual topics. We even roomed together on a mission trip to Dayton, Ohio. We had a great time together. Then, it just sort of faded into oblivion. Our friendship didn't last the year.

Why? I'm not sure, but I think it was the trash-talking. We were constantly teasing one another, picking at one another's words, ideas, faults, or quirks. I think, eventually, it ceased to be a pleasant experience being together and whether it was a conscious decision or not, we drifted to other people. He was my friend and I lost him because I never built him up; I never encouraged him. Today, I have no clue where he lives, or even if he is alive. When I think of him, I have regrets.

The flaming arrows of our constant trash-talking murdered our friendship—but, I was only joking.

I have to wonder what might have happened if I had been encouraging, instead. What if I had taken an interest in his life? What if I'd lifted him up instead of always trying to one-up his comments to me? It was all in fun, but in the end, it just wasn't fun.

Paul teaches us to let nothing unwholesome leave our mouths. Rather, he said to build one another up, to meet needs, and to benefit others who hear our words. I'm not very good at fulfilling that instruction, especially when it comes to my closest friends. I don't think I've learned my lesson.

I said in chapter one that words matter, and that is true whether we are speaking to a stranger or we are speaking to our closest friend. To love (*agape*) those closest to us, we need to be considerate of them, mindful of their needs, thoughtful of their feelings, and work to build them up. We should want to strengthen their hearts, lighten their loads, and unhitch guilt from their soul.

Loving others is not easy—even those closest to us. It takes work—mindful, intentional work. Think about your interactions with your friends. Are you a balm to their heart or a thorn in their foot?

Discussion Questions

1. Have you witnessed trash-talking in the sports world? Share about what you saw and how you felt about it.
2. Is trash-talking in a game okay? Why or why not?
3. Have you ever experienced trash-talking in a friendship? How did it make you feel?
4. Why is it so easy to trash-talk and so hard to be encouraging?
5. Take a few minutes and share encouraging words to one another in your discussion

group. If you need some help, maybe try filling in the blanks in the following sentences:

"I really appreciate it when you..."
"You have a real talent for..."
"It really moved me when you said..."
"One thing about you that I'd like to imitate is..."

Challenge

This week, be mindful of your words to your friends. Make a conscious effort to only say encouraging, beneficial words that will build your friends up.

Thirteen

Tom and Roland

Protectors in the Fray

Love...always protects,... I Corinthians 13:7 (NIV)
"Greater love has no one than this: to lay down one's life for one's friends." John 15:13 (NIV)

Incredible acts of heroism are rare and that is what makes them so amazing. Everyday there are situations that call for heroism, but in reality, few of us are often up to the task. A couple of weeks prior to the writing of this chapter, there was a school shooting in Noblesville, Indiana where a hero teacher charged and tackled the gunman, taking three bullet wounds in the process. On the other hand, in another recent school shooting, a police officer stayed outside allowing the shooter free reign inside until reinforcements arrived. I don't want to condemn the officer too harshly because I'm not sure what I would have done. Would I have had the courage to take action? Would you? I'd like to think I'd step up and act, but the fact is that I've never been much of a hero, neither in big things nor in little ones.

Those opportunities to show high profile heroism are publicized in the media to the extent that we think they are before us all the time, but the truth is that they are rare in our everyday lives. We rarely have the opportunity to protect someone in a big way, a publicly obvious way. The smaller opportunities are there, though. We each have the chance to protect one another in smaller ways—all the time. Maybe a co-worker is accused of some mistake that you know was not their fault—do you step in? A friend is spreading gossip about a mutual friend—do you shut it down? The blood bank is calling for donations—do you give? Someone is being abused because of their race, gender, or orientation—do you stop it? Or, do you join in?

I've never been much of a fighter. As a young person, I was truly afraid. I didn't want to get hurt. Generally, I avoided fights whenever possible, and I can only recall two scuffles and one real fight in the totality of my childhood. All three events involved the same boy—one of my childhood best friends. I would alter my routes, stay inside, leave early, and stay late — pretty much whatever it took to reduce the chances of a fight. On the other hand, I have a nephew who took to fighting like a fish to water. He is only four years younger than me, so he hit high school right after I graduated. He was one of those guys who didn't dance around, posturing, playing head games with the other guy. If someone started something, David just finished it. Boom. Bam. Done. My point here is not to encourage fighting. Rather, I'm just pointing out that some have more aggressive natures, while some of us are more timid when it comes to conflict. I have always been more timid.

You could say that I'm not fond of conflict. I tend to avoid it. If something was going down out in the street, I'd be more likely to call the police and wait than to run out and step into the fray.

Paul said that love always protects. Jesus said that there is no greater love than when someone puts themselves at risk for their friends—to the point of death. Isn't that exactly what Jesus did? The bottom line is that sometimes, you've got to be willing to put yourself on the line if you really want to love.

Two good examples were set for me in the fall of 1981 in the parking lot beside the church and Christian School I was associated with during my two years of Bible College. A bunch of us guys, some college students and some high school students, were playing basketball at a hoop that had been set up on one side of the lot, opposite the main buildings. At one point, the play was interrupted when a boy from town, not associated with the school or the church, approached one of the Christian School boys and wanted to fight. I don't really recall the reason, but it was likely over a girl. The aggressor was a big guy, much bigger and more aggressive than the kid he wanted to fight.

Tom stepped in. He was my age, but a touch smaller than me. Actually, he was smaller than the aggressive town boy, too. However, Tom wasn't about to let that kid beat up on the smaller boy. Instead, he stepped between them, grabbed the larger boy by the collar and pulled his right hand back—cocked and ready to rock. "Give me a reason," Tom said, over and over. "Give me a reason!" What I haven't told you yet, is that Tom has a disabled right hand that was damaged in a traffic accident when he was three years old. Regardless, he ran the aggressor off and protected the high school kid. No punches were thrown, and no one got hurt. I was amazed at Tom's actions.

However, that wasn't the end of the story.

Fifteen or maybe thirty minutes later, we were all still out there playing basketball, maybe six of us, when we noticed several large young men on motorcycles gathering out by the road. We could see them between the edge of the parking lot and Mr. Wise's home. Roland Wise lived with his wife and daughters in a small house just off the side of the parking lot. These guys with the motorcycles were big, definitely bigger than us.

They were standing out there making plans, pointing at each of us, deciding who was going to take who. Tom had run one off, but the boy had returned with his back up. It was going to go down, and there was no getting out of it. I wasn't going to run, but it sure didn't look like it was going to end well for us. Did I mention that they were big guys?

After they had their plan set and each of us picked out for annihilation, they started up into the grass between the parking lot and Mr. Wise's house. That was when Roland's back door opened, and he stepped out. He was a full grown, mature man. He wasn't the rag tag bunch of Bible College students or Christian High School boys they expected to face. He stepped around the corner of his house and took up a position between the larger boys and us. He then crossed his arms and said with a booming voice: "Hello boys."

"Uh, hello Mr. Wise," they hesitantly replied. Immediately, they began to backpedal. Basically, they turned and fled.

I never saw them again. It was over. Roland had stepped up and protected us—literally.

I'm sure that when he was looking out his window at the throw down that was about to occur, he didn't think: *Hey! I better go show those guys some agape love!* Still, that is what he did. When he stepped out of his back door, he was choosing to provide for us what we could not provide for ourselves—protection. In that moment, he demonstrated a self-sacrificing *agape* love. The truth is, as big as Roland Wise was, those boys could have taken him out and still come after us. He didn't know they would back down. Still, he was willing to step into the fray to protect us. It's a good thing for us that he didn't have my timid nature.

There is no room in love for fear. Well-formed love banishes fear. Since fear is crippling, a fearful life—fear of death, fear of judgement—is one not yet fully formed in love. 1 John 4:18 (The Message)

It is my goal that as I grow in the love of God

for others, I will be more and more willing to step into the fray and be a shield of protection to those who cannot protect themselves. It is my goal that I won't let potential damage to my reputation, damage to my career, damage to my church responsibility, or even physical pain prevent me from protecting someone—anyone—who would need my help. I cannot claim to love others if I am not willing to stand as a protector before them, even my enemies.

Discussion Questions

1. Share about someone who is being hailed as a hero in the news.
2. Share about a time when someone stepped up to protect you.
3. Do you have more of a tendency to fight or to avoid conflicts? Why?
4. What are some examples of how Christians could be more involved in protecting those who need help?
5. What keeps us from stepping into the fray? Should those things keep us from stepping in?

Challenge

Being mindful of those you are around and interact with this week, look for ways to step in and be a protector.

Fourteen

Angel in 22D

Love...it is not self-seeking... 1 Corinthians 13:5 (NIV)

As Jesus approached Jericho, a blind man was sitting by the roadside begging. When he heard the crowd going by, he asked what was happening. They told him, "Jesus of Nazareth is passing by."

He called out, "Jesus, Son of David, have mercy on me!"

Those who led the way rebuked him and told him to be quiet, but he shouted all the more, "Son of David, have mercy on me!"

Jesus stopped and ordered the man to be brought to him. When he came near, Jesus asked him, "What do you want me to do for you?"

"Lord, I want to see," he replied.

Jesus said to him, "Receive your sight; your faith has healed you." Luke 18:35-42 (NIV)

Over Labor Day weekend a few years ago, my wife and I took an extra day off of work and flew to Denver to visit some friends. It was a fantastic time, a time of laughter, good food, and relaxation. We took in the Allison Krause and Union Station concert at Red Rocks. We drove up to our friends' cabin in the mountains. We hiked the Garden of the Gods. We saw Boulder. We saw Golden. We held our niece's baby, our great niece. We had a wonderful time.

The flight out to Denver was uneventful, just the way you prefer that a flight be. We moved smoothly through security without the need of a personal pat-down, our flight took off and landed on time, and our friend was there to meet us.

It was the flight home that I'd like to share about.

Before I get to that, I want to say that I must have one of those faces. Some people have faces that others would just as soon avoid. Scary faces. Mean faces. Faces that make you want to look the other way. Others have pretty faces. Faces that attract attention because of their beauty. I guess I have a face that makes people want to talk.

It's not really new to me. I'm sort of getting used to it. Sometimes I go into a brand new restaurant and say "hi" to the waitress, and the next thing I know, she's filled me in on the details of her life like where she's from, why she's where she's at, and what she'd like to become. I learn about the family dog and where the person went to college. Stuff like that.

Sometimes it's ordinary stuff. Sometimes it's difficult stuff, stuff that breaks people down. Stuff that will break your heart.

Once, on a flight home from Albany, New

York, I caught a connecting flight in Detroit. The guy in the seat next to mine started talking to me as we taxied to take off, and he stopped talking to me as we exited the plane in Indy. He shared that he and his wife were separated. She'd had an affair with one of his friends whom he had invited to stay with them. He claimed that he himself was to blame because he had gotten caught up with porn. By the time we were done talking, I knew all about his profession and the business he owned. I knew why he was coming to Indiana, and I knew that he still loved his wife despite the mess.

I wish I could say that I really helped that guy. I don't know if I did anything for him beyond providing a compassionate ear. I tried to encourage him to look to God, but what else could I really do? He gave me his email address and I did reach out to him later, but he never responded. You know, though, that sometimes all people really need is someone that will truly listen. I did give him that.

When I look back on all of the random conversations I've had with strangers, I don't really know why people feel so free to talk to me. Perhaps, it is a gift. I have friends that I sit down with at lunch, and the next thing they know, they are telling me stuff. I've had customers to spill their personal lives into my lap. I've come to expect it. It just happens, and usually I am happy to listen and if needed, I try to help.

But, sometimes, I just don't want it to happen.

Sometimes, I just want to relax. Sometimes, I just want to enjoy a trip with my wife.

Back to my flight home from Denver. We were

in the terminal and we were early, so we found some seats facing our gate. My wife sat down first at the end of a row, there was an open seat for me next to her and then there was a seat that had a guy's stuff on it. The guy with the stuff was in the next seat after that. He was taking up a bit of space. Being courteous, I said hello as I sat down.

I guess that opened the door.

He started talking to me. He said he flew a lot. He told me that he had been in the military, a Marine. He used to be married, but he left when his wife got bossy. His brother was still in the military. He was coming to Indiana to go on a religious retreat. He thought Eli Manning was a much better quarterback than Peyton Manning. On and on.

He also fidgeted a lot. He couldn't sit still very long, and kept rubbing his face, smoothing his straggly beard. It didn't take me very long to decide that he didn't have all his mental screws tightened down. I don't mean to be flippant about mental illness. My comment here is meant to convey my reaction to him in that moment, a reaction that I'm not proud of, and is not reflective of any disregard of the seriousness of the problems that so many people face.

He made me feel uncomfortable.

I really just didn't want to talk to him, but I didn't want to be rude either. I didn't want to outright shut him down. However, I also didn't want to encourage the conversation, so I didn't carry the discussion forward. I didn't ask any questions. I only spoke in response to something he would say or ask. I began to give him abbreviated responses, yes and no answers. I turned forward to ensure my body language sent the message that I didn't want to talk. I kept hoping he would sort of understand that I didn't want to converse. Despite my stoicism, he kept talking to me.

Silently, I said a little prayer...

"Please God, don't let him sit next to me on the plane."

You're probably thinking something like: *Oh, you shouldn't have done that.* You would be right. There were dozens of people on that flight. It was full. The chances of him sitting next to me were probably better than 100 to 1, but I knew as soon as I said that silent prayer that he would be right next to me.

My seat was 22C. It wasn't five minutes later that I learned that his seat was 22D. He was directly beside me, across the aisle.

Maybe I should have gotten the hint from that fact, but I still didn't want to talk to him. I was stubborn, maybe a little like Jonah. I wanted to do what I wanted to do. I had my own selfish agenda.

Our flight boarded. I sat down. He sat down. I was sort of in luck in that there were two cute young women who were sitting on the other side of him. They drew some of his attention away. I felt kind of lucky, but I also felt kind of guilty.

Still, I didn't want to talk to him. So, I took the freebee ear-buds that Frontier Airlines gave us so we could hear the sound from their little seatback TVs, and I put one in my ear on his side to discourage him from bothering me. Over the next couple of hours, I watched a little TV, I read my book, and I ignored the slightly off-kilter guy in 22D.

For the most part it worked. He only nudged my arm a few times during the flight. The rest of the time he sat and fidgeted, or talked to the girls. I flew in peace, and….

…I failed the test.

When you think through this whole thing, does it really sound to you like a coincidence? I mean, what are the chances? I already shared the odds. You might call it Karma, but I call it God.

Now, maybe he was just a slightly wacked out former serviceman suffering the side effects of serving his country. Maybe he was just a simple, struggling human to whom my heart should have gone out. Or, maybe he was something more. There's just something about this thing that's been gnawing at me.

Consider Hebrews 13:2 (NIV).

"Do not forget to show hospitality to strangers, for by so doing some people have shown hospitality to angels without knowing it."

Would it have been so bad to have spent some time talking to him? Could I have opened my heart up to a stranger and made him feel safe and cared about? Could I have taken some of the burden off of the two young college-age girls who sat on his other side? Did he simply need a friendly ear?

Would it have been too much to ask of me to sacrifice a little bit of my personal satisfaction on a two and a half hour flight home? In retrospect, I think not. Instead of giving, I withheld. Instead of reaching out, I withdrew. Instead of acting out of compassion, I reacted out of my selfish desire for my personal space. I failed. I failed to love.

My "angel" in 22D is still on my mind. He reminds me that I have some growing to do—in compassion—and, in dealing with my own personal selfishness. I plan to watch for him on future flights, at the table across from me in the restaurant, or in the eyes of the homeless person sitting on the curb. Perhaps, you should watch for him, too.

Next time, I'll do better.

Discussion Questions

1. Can you share about a time when you really needed someone to listen to you?
2. If you experienced a time when someone really gave you their ear, how did that make you feel?
3. Why do you think that people avoid taking the time to listen to others?
a. People they know?
b. Strangers?
4. What gift or gifts do you have that could be sent by God to help others around you?
5. Consider Matthew 25:14-30. What is the danger of not using God's gifts that were meant to benefit others?

Challenge

Pay attention to the attributes of your character that can be utilized to help others. Look for ways to use the gift or gifts that God has provided you to benefit others.

Fifteen

An Unknown Cousin

Words without Life
Context

So in everything, do to others what you would have them do to you, for this sums up the Law and the Prophets. Matthew 7:12 (NIV)

Jesus replied: "'Love the Lord your God with all your heart and with all your soul and with all your mind.' This is the first and greatest commandment. And the second is like it: 'Love your neighbor as yourself.' All the Law and the Prophets hang on these two commandments." Matthew 22:37-40 (NIV)

Not long ago, I attended a graduation reception for a young man. He had sent me an invitation through Facebook. He is the adopted son of a couple that my wife and I were friends with at the congregation where we had attended for many years before moving on over a decade ago. I hadn't seen any of the family for several years, so when I got the invitation, I decided to go to both support the young man and to maybe reconnect a bit with our friends. Overall, it was a friendly visit, but there was one interaction that stood out.

The family was friendly, yet a little surprised when I appeared at their door. It was fun to reconnect, and I had a pleasant visit with them and with some other friends I had not seen for many years. At one point, I was chatting with one of those friends when another guy I hadn't seen for more than a decade arrived. He was a little surprised to see me also, so he came over to say hello.

"Last time I saw you," he said, "you had some sort of back problem. You were all laid back in a Lazyboy chair."

"Wow," I replied. "That must have been 2005 when I had the herniated disk in my neck."

That meant that it had been about thirteen years since our last encounter, at least the last one that either of us recalled. Not much more was said and he moved on to talk with other people at the party.

Before I go on with the end of this story, let me give you a little background. In 2005, I was planning a hiking and rafting trip to the Grand Canyon with my oldest daughter, so I had been working out rather intensely to prepare for the adventure. At the time of my disk injury, I was about forty pounds lighter than I am right now. His last vision of me in his mind was one that was younger, leaner, active, and more physically fit.

Over the interceding years, I've been like a yoyo with my weight and fitness going up and down. I've been lighter than he had last seen me and I've been heavier than I am right now. Also, since the day that man saw me lounging in the chair, I've had life happen to me with sickness, leg injuries, surgeries, deaths, and job adjustments. Both my daughters have gone off to college, graduated, and moved on into career paths. Basically, a lot has happened, and he wasn't privy to any of it because we didn't have any interaction or relationship during that time. Our lives had been completely disconnected from one another.

I hung around for about another thirty minutes, maybe forty-five and then I decided to take my leave. I wandered over to the table where the host was seated to say goodbye, and the man who had mentioned my injury was seated there also. He looked over to me and had one more question:

"So, Mike, have you not been doing anything since your neck injury?"

Wow. Boy. Really? Good to see you, too. Those were the thoughts that shot through my mind. I was more than happy to leave at that point. Frankly, it hurt and I felt embarrassed. His comment was probably spoken very innocently and meant to express concern. Maybe it was just awkwardly phrased. In my insecurity, I likely took it out of context. After all, I do know him to be a kind and good-hearted person. Still, the lack of relationship combined with my own issues gave those words an edge that wasn't intended.

***

As I typed them into my laptop, I noticed a corollary between the two verses that I shared in the heading of this chapter. I'd never before noticed it. Maybe you have, but it just struck me. Jesus ends Matthew 22:40 with: "All the Law and the Prophets <u>hang on these two commandments."</u> Earlier, he had ended Matthew 7:12 with: "...for this <u>sums up the Law and the Prophets."</u>

Did you see that? Jesus connects the love of God, the love of neighbor, and what we have commonly called the Golden Rule. Treating others the way that you want to be treated is directly attached to loving God and loving those around you. That means that it is of the utmost importance that we are incredibly thoughtful in our interactions and our words—whether verbal or written, spoken or on social media.

***

If you've read all the way to here, then you know that I've not always been too great at being incredibly thoughtful. I want to share another of my failures now, but one that takes a different angle than my previous debacles. Like the guy earlier, I had the best of intentions. I meant no ill will. I was speaking from concern.

My dad had nine siblings and unfortunately, I didn't get to know all of them very well. One in particular, I may have only met once because she and her family lived in Arizona while I grew up in Indiana. They rarely made the journey home for our family gatherings that were held near Lima, Ohio. Further, my dad was about fifty years old when I was born, so most of my cousins were older than me. Some of the cousins that were more my age were actually the children of my first cousins.

When I was about thirteen or fourteen, we had a family reunion in Ohio. I'm not sure if it was purely a reunion or maybe a time when the family gathered for a funeral. In my memory, it feels happy, like a reunion but a lot of time has gone by. At this particular event, the family from Arizona attended and I had the chance to meet some more cousins that I had not previously known. So far, so good.

One of those young cousins was maybe a couple of years younger than me, and she was quite overweight for a young teen. I befriended her and we talked, played some games, and had reunion food. At some point, my heart went out to her due to her weight. In my memory, I see a flushed face and sweat on her cheeks. I was genuinely concerned about her, wishing her the best in life. I had no intention of teasing her, belittling her, or shaming her in any way. I wanted to help her.

I don't remember what I said exactly, I just know that it wasn't taken the way that I intended to deliver it. It was probably something like: "I bet if you keep playing as hard as we have today, you can lose a bunch of that weight."

She stopped whatever we were doing, looked at me briefly with her eyes welling up with tears, and then ran off crying. She wouldn't talk to me after that, and I have never seen her since that day. I don't even know her name. Another potentially great relationship burned by my careless words—regardless of the fact that they were good-intentioned.

My problem wasn't that I was trying to be funny and I certainly wasn't trying to be hurtful. Rather, my problem was that I was trying to be helpful without a relationship. I thought that my two hours at the family reunion gave me enough knowledge to speak into her twelve years of life. I had no way to know that my words would hurt so much because I didn't really know her. I didn't know her pain. I didn't know her health. I didn't know what other kids did or said to her. Because of my thoughtlessness, I never would know those things.

If I had taken the time to put myself into her position, to consider her point of view, I could have avoided that disaster. That is the point of "doing to others what you would have them do to you." If we will take the time to consider how our words might feel, or how our actions would affect us if we were on the receiving end, we would often likely alter what we plan to say or do.

For example, consider if you had been away from church for a while, feeling guilty and maybe feeling really nervous about a return, but as you were walking in, someone playfully says: "I haven't seen you in a while. Where have you been?" or "It's not Christmas or Easter, what brings you here?" In reality, your response to those questions would depend on the relationship. If it were a close friend, someone who has been in the trenches with you, you'd probably laugh it off. However, if it were a casual acquaintance or maybe someone that you're only distantly familiar with, you'd very possibly turn around and leave. The relationship makes all the difference.

You can say hard (loving) things to people with whom you have done the hard work of building a relationship. Short of that, sometimes it is better to just keep your words to yourself. Instead, put your arms around them and start the connection with some affection.

I'll leave you with this truism from Theodore Roosevelt: *"Nobody cares how much you know until they know how much you care."*

Discussion Questions

1. Share about a time when someone with good intentions hurt you with their words nonetheless.
2. Share about a time when someone you were close with said something hard to you that you appreciated. Why were you able to accept the hard words from them?
3. Have you ever inadvertently said something hurtful when you were only trying to help?
4. How does social media (Facebook, Twitter, etc.) come into play? If we are to apply the Golden Rule to our interactions on social media, would it change what you post?
5. How is the Golden Rule interrelated with the Greatest Commandments?

Challenge

Before you post anything on social media this week, stop and consider how your words might affect someone else.

Bonus Challenge

Whenever you see someone this week and you are tempted to share some "helpful" life tips, first consider how you can build a better relationship with him or her.

Sixteen

Lovementalism

Flip the Script

"Do not judge, or you too will be judged. For in the same way you judge others, you will be judged, and with the measure you use, it will be measured to you." Matthew 7:1-2 (NIV)

Who are you to judge someone else's servant? To their own master, servants stand or fall. And they will stand, for the Lord is able to make them stand. Romans 14:4 (NIV)

For we must all appear before the judgment seat of Christ, so that each of us may receive what is due us for the things done while in the body, whether good or bad. 2 Corinthians 5:10 (NIV)

And over all these virtues put on love, which binds them all together in perfect unity. Colossians 3:14 (NIV)

Love never fails. 1 Corinthians 13:8 (NIV)

"That means it works every time it's tried."

John Wright

If you only had this book to go by, you'd think that the loving folks I've highlighted in the previous chapters were some sort of super Christ-followers who had it together in some nearly supernatural way. Further, you'd think that I'm just a dolt without any sense of tact or thoughtfulness at all. The truth is that those folks had or have their weak spots, and I'm not nearly as bad as those specific instances might imply. We are all imperfect creatures tasked by God with learning to love the way that he does. He knows we mess up. That's what grace is for.

A few years ago, my wife and I and our two daughters took a trip to Chicago. We rode the Megabus. I got a little nervous as we boarded when I saw that the bus was going to be piloted into the heavy Chicago traffic by a young, African-American woman, but regardless, I put my life and the life of my family into her hands. (I bet that last sentence made you uncomfortable. It did me, too. More on that in a bit.)

It was a pleasant extended weekend where we ate some good food and toured some interesting places. We did a lot of walking and staring and eating and browsing and general sight-seeing. It was fun with one major exception: my wife got a nasty little cold. She was stuffy and flushed, and generally did not feel good, but she was a trooper and hung with us. She's tougher than me; that's for sure.

On the last evening of our visit to the windy city, we decided we needed to indulge in some

Chicago-style pizza, so we walked about a mile to a downtown Giordano's Pizzeria. The place was packed with about an hour wait, so we took our little buzzer thing and waited outside.

Nancy's face was even more flushed from the walk and her eyes were watering. It was a head cold, so she looked worse than she felt. Still, she definitely didn't feel good.

As we stood there in the crowd waiting, we noticed a homeless woman working her way toward us. She hit up a number of other patrons along the way, but she eventually arrived at our little group of four huddled near the door. At the time, I looked at her like she was a fly that needed to be shooshed away. She was dirty and ragged. My fear instinct kicked in. *What if she is high on something?* I thought. *Is she a pickpocket? Will she leave quickly or bother us until we give her something?* Have you been there? Do you understand what I was doing?

She stepped up to us and promptly flipped the script. She took one look at my wife's watery eyes and flushed face, and instead of asking me for money, she went to the defense of my bride. "Have you been hurting her?" she asked me. She was glaring at me. "Is he harming you?" she asked Nancy. "You better not be hitting this lady!" she said, turning back to me.

Of course, my wife assured her that I was not abusing her and that she simply had a cold. "Are you sure?" she asked again. Then she looked at me again, doubt in her eyes. "You treat her right!" Shortly after, she moved on and we feasted on pizza, but I will always remember that homeless person who had my wife's back. She misjudged the situation, but she acted out of love and concern. Me, on the other hand, I had judged her all up and down before she reached us. Dirty clothes. Dirty face. Dirty hair. A bit of an odor. She was begging for money. I moved on to my own set of assumptions. Alcoholic? Addict? Thief? Mentally unstable?

Which one of us acted out of love?

Let's consider something that hits us all in one way or another. It's something that I think is particularly the antithesis of love. It is our tendency to judge. Judgmentalism. We do it every time we look at someone. It's a subconscious thing. To defeat it, we have to consciously deny it any space.

We judge based on skin color, long hair, short hair, tattoos, clothing styles, jobs, neighborhoods, religious background, gender, lifestyle, how fast someone drives, how slowly someone drives, age, education, movie choices, marital status, divorce, sense of humor, and I could go on, and on, and on. I judged that bus driver when we boarded the Megabus. Was my concern that she was black, or that she was young, or that she was a woman? Would I have felt better if she was an older black woman? What if she were a young white woman? A young black man? Was my prejudice based on race, gender, or age? A combination? I don't really know. I just know it was there, it was completely unwarranted, and I'm ashamed of it. She did a fine job maneuvering that giant vehicle through the metropolitan traffic.

I bet you've done something similar.

Have you ever called another driver an idiot

because they did something in traffic that irritated you? You have? See, you looked at what they did and judged them an idiot.

A man stands up in church to confess to a struggle in his life and suddenly the women begin to avoid him. Somehow, they judge him dangerous. A woman confesses a struggle and the whispers begin. She is judged to be sinful and a bad example. Insert whichever struggle you can think of and the response is the same. We throw our noses up in judgement rather than throwing our arms open in love.

Seriously. We do it all the time. That man's clothes are threadbare. That woman's skirt is too short. That neighbor doesn't cut his grass enough. That other one doesn't care enough to spray the weeds. She's got a potty mouth. He works too much. He doesn't seem to want to work.

All of these "judgments" get in the way of our being able to see people for who they are: God's loved children—folks for whom he bled and died. It causes us to avoid people. It makes us fearful. It makes us uncomfortable. Judgmentalism sucks the life out of our relationships like a spiritual vampire and we need to stake it in the heart.

However, it's not enough to simply stop judging others. That judgmental attitude has to be replaced. Something has to fill the void it leaves in our hearts when we kick it to the curb. Consider Matthew 12:43-45: *"When an impure spirit comes out of a person, it goes through arid places seeking rest and does not find it. Then it says, 'I will return to the house I left.' When it arrives, it finds the house unoccupied, swept clean and put in order. Then it goes and takes with it seven other spirits more wicked than itself, and they go in and live there. And the final condition of that person is worse than the first. That is how it will be with this wicked generation."* (NIV)

We can't just kick that judgmental spirit to the curb and expect it not to return. We have to find a new occupant. We need to replace judgmentalism with a better occupant. Lovementalism.

I like to make up words and this is one of my favorites. Here's how I define it:

Lovementalism (noun) —A predisposition to love people regardless of who they are, where they are from, and what they are like. The embodiment of the biblical concept of *agape* love.

It's time to start intentionally loving people.

The Bible says that God is love. It also says that God is light—in him there is no darkness at all. *The light shines in the darkness, and the darkness has not overcome it.* John 1:5 (NIV) I believe that God's love also shines in the darkness, and the darkness does not overcome it either. *Love never fails.*

God loves the people he has made. All of them. A whole world of them. He died for them. Who am I to judge them? You know that scruffy, dirty guy on the curb with the sign and the little plastic cup? God loves him. You know that hard-drinking, chain-smoking, obscenity-slinging, bar-hopper? God loves her. You know that self-righteous, pious, stiff-necked Bible-thumper? God loves him. You know that obnoxious, politics-driven, statehouse-marching activist? Yep, God loves her.

There is a judgment seat and it belongs to someone other than me. Have you ever mistakenly taken someone's seat only to have them come and glare at you? Awkward. I imagine that Christ feels pretty particular about who sits in his seat, too. I'd rather not have Him come and glare at me.

Love never fails.

My friend, John Wright says that little phrase from 1 Corinthians 13 means that "it works every time it's tried." When I look around at the world that surrounds me, at the TV news and the social media feeds, it seems to me that we aren't trying it nearly enough.

Are you willing to give lovementalism a try? God hung everything on love. Shouldn't you and I follow suit? Flip the script. Stop judging and start loving. ***Love never fails.***

Discussion Questions

1. If people judged you on your worst moments, what would they say?
2. Have you ever been misjudged? Share about it.
3. Describe the little ways that you tend to judge others.
4. Which is easier? To love people or to judge people? Why?
5. How does love shine into the darkness?
6. Create a definition for "lovementalism." What does it mean to you?

Challenge

I've been told that it takes repetition to change a habit. You have to make the change and then repeat it over and over again until the bad habit is gone and a new habit is in its place. Flip the script. Therefore, for the last challenge, I want to give you something that will take you a few weeks into the future, something that may assist you in creating an attitude of lovementalism. I urge you to take up the Lovementalism Challenge.

The Lovementalism Challenge

		Scripture	Meditation	Challenge
Sun		Matthew 22:34-40	Contemplate God's patience and grace in your life	Connect face to face with at least one neighbor
Mon		Matthew 5:43-48	Contemplate the power and strength of God as it relates to things that you fear	Take a step to reconcile a broken relationship in your life
Tues		Matthew 25:31-46	Consider how important meeting tangible needs is in the grand scheme of things	Look for a way to meet a need today
Wed		John 13:1-17, 34-35	Washing another's feet is a choice. Consider	Large or small, find a way to be a servant

		whether you are making choices to serve others in the family of God. How have others gone out of their way to serve you?	today
Th ur	John 15:9-17	Do you have "friends" in Christ that you are willing to lay down your life for? Who? What are you doing to build those friendships?	Invest in a Christian friend today. Call or visit. Share from your life and ask about theirs.
Fri	Galatia ns 5:2-6	Controve rsies are always vying for our attention and captivating our minds. What	Intention ally find a way to share your faith *through love* with someone today. Do

		spiritual controversies attract your attention? Do these controversies sometimes undermine your love for others?	something tangible for someone that will reflect positively on your faith in Christ.
Sat	Ephesians 4:1-7	"Bear with one another" "Make every effort to keep the unity" "But to each of us grace has been given…" Some people are difficult and hard to put up with. Do you bear with them in love? Do you allow them the grace that Christ has	Spend time in prayer for a difficult person. If possible, look for a way to be a blessing to them today.

		apportioned?	

Instructions:

      1. Either in groups or individually, commit to repeating this devotional for four weeks

      2. Write down your thoughts for each day

      3. At the end of the four weeks, compare each week's thoughts to see how your thinking and your actions have developed

      4. Write a final statement of how the challenge affected you

      5. Have your group share with each other throughout the process and share the final statements together

As an alternative, you could make each day's devotion a weekly devotion instead, repeating it daily until you have worked through all of the devotionals over the course of seven weeks.

Copyrights

Suggested Reading
Love Does: Discover a Secretly Incredible Life in an Ordinary World by Bob Goff
Everybody Always: Becoming Love in a World Full of Setbacks and Difficult People by Bob Goff
Love First: Ending Hate before It's Too Late by Don McLaughlin

Michael DeCamp has been in pursuit of God since he was a toddler. Over the decades he has been a bus kid, a youth group member, a Bible college student, a Bible study leader, a ministry intern, a small group leader, a youth director, and a church elder. He has also been a son, a brother, a husband, a father, an uncle, a neighbor, and an employee. Through the years, he has continued to pursue a deeper understanding of God's love for people. He is the father of two talented daughters, the husband of a brilliant woman, and the would-be master of one little, high-strung miniature Australian shepherd named Leo. He lives in Indianapolis and enjoys writing, podcasting, and taking cool vacations.

Made in the USA
Monee, IL
23 January 2020